Shin

MW01088955

Cherilynn Bistano

Shine, Don't Whine

Shine, Don't Whine

Cherrilynn Bisbano

CrossLink Publishing

CrossLink Publishing
1601 Mt. Rushmore Rd, STE 3288
Rapid City, SD 57702

Ordering Information:
Quantity sales. Special discounts are available on quantity purchases by corporations, associations, and others. For details, contact the "Special Sales Department" at the address above.

Shine, Don't Whine/Bisbano —1st ed.

ISBN 978-1-63357-214-0

Library of Congress Control Number: 2019954583

First edition: 10 9 8 7 6 5 4 3 2 1

Published in association with Cyle Young of the Hartline Literary Agency, LLC.

Contents

Pit of Perfection

"And you, who once were alienated and hostile in mind, doing evil deeds" (Colossians 1:21 ESV).

I sat in the nurse's office trying to explain the bruises and welts on the back of my legs. Third grade was difficult enough with the boys making fun of my freckles; now I had to explain the wounds. I thought all fathers beat their kids with a belt. After all, I was disobedient—I didn't make my bed to military specifications or wash dishes to his standards. I could never please my father. I was a bad girl.

I started my journey as a blonde, sun-kissed girl who loved dolls, cats, and climbing trees. I was a tomboy by day and a beautician by night. No tree went unclimbed, and my Barbie dolls had the latest hairdo and fashions.

Like most children, I tried to please my father. When I was four, my military dad wanted a quarter to bounce off the bed. I spent hours perfecting the creases, hospital corners, and tightness of the blankets—in hopes the quarter would bounce. Each time, he tore off all the linens and made me do it over. I prayed for the silver coin to jump off the mattress so I could go out and play Batman and Robin with the neighbor kids. The quarter never bounced, and he finally gave up.

"You won't amount to anything, Cherrilynn. You can't even make a bed. Get outside, you little monster."

I stood on a chair to wash dishes. My sisters and I rotated jobs of washing, drying, and putting dishes away. My dad walked into the kitchen as I scraped the egg off the pan with a metal spoon. I felt a slap upside my head.

"Ouch!" I thought my sister hit me.

"Don't talk back to me, and you never use metal on that pan. You are so stupid." He slapped me again.

The three of us held back tears as my dad grabbed a beer and walked out. We didn't want a beating for crying.

No matter how hard I tried, I could not make him happy.

Nothing made him happy. After nine years of mental, physical, and sexual abuse, my mother kicked him out and filed for divorce.

I saw my father one last time. He came to the apartment, but my mother wouldn't let him through the door.

"Cheryol, I want Cherrilynn to live with me. We know you cannot provide for all three girls," he said, eyes fixed on me.

"No, she will stay here with us."

"Don't you love Daddy? Don't you want to live with me, Cherrilynn?"

My heart broke. I did love my daddy. He asked for me specifically. I felt special. I longed to run into his arms and receive the love I had never experienced. My mother held me back and closed the door to what could have become a lifetime of abuse.

* * *

The degrading words of my father penetrated my heart and mind. "You're an animal." "You're stupid." Soon the memories confused my self-talk, and the self-talk became my reality: *My daddy hates me, so I'm worthless. I must be perfect for my daddy to love me—for anyone to love me. I will earn his love—and others' love. He won't come back—others will leave me too.*

Twenty-five years later, I learned my father had been a prisoner of war in Vietnam. My father witnessed hideous acts of violence that took the lives of his brothers-in-arms. My aunt told me that he became a medic to help people, and he found himself in the middle of a combat zone. The Vietnamese soldiers shot at him as he tried to rescue his brothers and board them on the helicopter. Instead of picking up his friends, he picked up an M-16 and, in his words, "murdered many enemy combatants." The Vietnamese captured him.

After his release, he came back angry and confused. We were his human punching bags. I learned a casualty of war is not only a person injured while serving our country, but also those who were and are affected by the servicemember's actions and words. The result: I became a wounded child enduring an inner battle to be perfect so my father would be happy—a war I could never win.

I pushed for perfection, and my pursuit continued through my teens and twenties. I strove to get the best grades, befriend the popular kids, and be the best person I could be. I was in bondage to an image I could never obtain.

Over time, striving for perfection took its toll on my body and my friendships. The stress of acting perfect, along with my rigorous flight schedule in the Navy, made my body and mind ill. People disliked me because I had to be the best. You may have encountered someone like me. A 95 percent on a test did not sit well with me. *Why didn't I get 100 percent? I didn't study hard enough. I'm a failure.* I argued with the teachers. Many times, I proved the original question was flawed, and I won points for my classmates and me. But at what cost? I felt empty because I had not achieved perfection the first time.

***

Shine, Don't Whine is my journey to know perfection—not my ideal perfection, not my dad's definition or anyone else's, but God's perfection. I never have and never will achieve perfection this side of heaven. Now perfection, Jesus Christ, the one who is perfect, knows me and continues to deliver me from the chains that bind me—the bondage of complaining and wrongful thinking.

God has redirected my path, and I no longer need to strive for the unobtainable. He rescued me from the pit of self-absorption. All my longing for acceptance, accolades, and love are now met in Jesus. My destination is no longer impossible; my destination is Jesus. In Jesus, we can all be satisfied, whole—perfect.

There were times during my journey I thought I knew better than God; after all, I lived my life without him for twenty-eight years. One father had already let me down. Could I trust my heavenly Father?

God patiently waited as I learned the hard way. I tried to use my knowledge and strength to solve my problems. I did not ask God for help. I just complained about my situation. My stubbornness and lack of trust in God led me down painful paths. Pity and self-reliance remained my close friends. I was comfortable with my dysfunction—until the Word convicted me: "Do everything without grumbling or arguing, so that you may become blameless and pure, 'children of God without fault in a warped and crooked generation.' Then you will shine among them like **stars** in the sky" (Philippians 2:14–15 NIV).

I desired to shine like a star for the Lord and stop whining. A friend confirmed the Word's conviction.

"Cherrilynn, you certainly complain a lot," she said. The truth hurt. I knew I needed to allow God to work in me.

Perhaps you too are longing for the freedom that comes when God's light shines in the dark dungeon of the soul but are too afraid to begin the journey. I remained fearful of rejection, but desperately desired God's guidance. I made many mistakes, but God guided me through them.

One day at work, I was ridiculed by a few coworkers because I said I was offended by their dirty jokes.

I found a quiet corner to sulk. Eyes were still on me.

My heart broke. They knew I was a Christian. Why would they say such nasty things in my presence, then make fun of me?

The taunts continued.

"Oh, Cherrilynn's here!" Mike said. "We'd better be good; she'll tell God on us."

"God wouldn't like our jokes either, would he?" Steve said.

"You guys are idiots!" I said as I left the room.

Laughter echoed throughout the office and followed me down the hallway as I escaped their harassment.

I prayed and asked for wisdom, but I really wanted God to call down lightning on them.

The Holy Spirit impressed this verse upon my heart instead: "For we are the aroma of Christ to God among those who are being saved and among those who are perishing" (2 Corinthians 2:15).

The Spirit continued, *Your choice is to whine or be wine when you are crushed. Do you want to complain or be a fragrant aroma? Do you want to shine, not whine?*

I returned to the office.

"I'm sorry for calling you idiots."

Mike and Steve's mouths opened wider than their eyes.

"We thought you'd never talk to us again," Mike said with his Cheshire grin.

"We accept the apology; we will warn you next time we tell those kinds of jokes," Steve said.

"Thanks, guys," I said.

After the apology, the dirty jokes stopped. They even came to me privately to ask for prayer.

I'm not always a fragrant offering when I go through trials and tribulations, but God is there to lovingly remind me that he will use the light of his Word to penetrate the dark places and dissolve my sin of complaining and wrong thinking.

My emotional and spiritual survival depends on God's promise to never leave during difficult times. He never did and never will. His commitment is for you too.

* * *

Now that you know a little bit about me, will you dare to join me and dive into the darkness? The journey of healing may be scary, but I encourage you to take the journey with me as we travel to those unfamiliar places together with God.

Do you want freedom? It is God's intent for us. "It was for freedom that Christ set us free; therefore keep standing firm and do not be subject again to a yoke of slavery" (Galatians 5:1 NASB).

Nothing worth having comes easily. Likewise, this journey requires work. A willing mind and heart are the most important. Please join me; we can find healing together.

Let's break free from the bondage of perfectionism and sin so we can transform into the likeness of the perfect one, Jesus, who is the light of the world. He is our destination. Let's continue to say goodbye to complaining, worry, doubt, and self-hatred. God has something beautiful in store, but we must allow him to shine his light so we can be light in the world.

Bible verses will be plentiful throughout this book. The English Standard Version (ESV) is used unless otherwise noted. The Word of God works with the Holy Spirit to change us from the inside out—to make us like Jesus. I call the process spiritual surgery.

Are you ready to surrender and allow God to go deep into the dark places? Remember, he already knows what lingers there. He promises to replace any void, wrong way of thinking, and pain with the light of his love. Will you join me on the journey to eradicate the sin that so easily entangles us so God can change our whine to shine? God will lead the way. Let's go!

* * *

To use *Shine, Don't Whine* as a Bible study:

- Read one chapter of the book a week.
- Memorize the Bible verse at the end of each chapter.
- Answer and discuss the light reflection questions.

==========================

Memory verse: Galatians 5:1
"It was for freedom that Christ set us free; therefore keep standing firm and do not be subject again to a yoke of slavery."

Light reflection questions

1. What lies do you believe about yourself?

2. What is one reason Christ came that is mentioned in this chapter?

3. When you get crushed, does God get wine or a whine? Explain.

Attitude Adjustment

*U*gh! *Morning? Again?* Pain permeated my body, and life's circumstances consumed my thoughts.

My husband was out of work. My son kicked, screamed, bit, and pulled the hair of other children at preschool because his autism hindered him from healthy communication. I didn't know how to help them and didn't have the energy to try.

Was failure stamped across my forehead? The continual ache in my muscles, along with fatigue and brain fog made me keenly aware that fibromyalgia and chronic fatigue syndrome (CFS) were overrunning my body again. I only had strength each day to either put the dishes in the dishwasher or fold a load of laundry. The thoughts in my brain were like the eggs I cooked for my son—scrambled. To grasp an idea and relay it verbally was like separating the yolk from the whites after they're combined. Impossible. Guilt provided a pity pool for me to swim in. I was one dilemma away from drowning.

I needed to swim, not sink, but I wasn't quite ready to tread water.

I need an attitude adjustment, Lord. I want to stop complaining and see your loving hand in every situation.

The Holy Spirit's voice echoed in my head, *Go to your Bible and look for the word "attitude!"* My body desired to remain in bed, but I knew I must obey.

I descended the stairs, poured my coffee, and began my study.

This verse came to mind before I opened my Bible, "Have this attitude in yourselves which was also in Christ Jesus" (Philippians 2:5 NASB).

Yes, Lord, I want the attitude of Christ.

The concordance showed sixteen verses containing the word "attitude" in the New English Translation (NET). This shocked me. Our attitude is vital to God.

The Greek word for "attitude," *phronéō*, means to exercise the mind.

Exercise meant work, and I was already exhausted. But I was determined to do whatever necessary to find joy, purpose, and peace.

I continued to read Philippians and found the verse that ignited the flame to write this book. The verse convicted and encouraged me. "Do everything without grumbling or arguing, so that you may become blameless and pure, 'children of God without fault in a warped and crooked generation.' Then you will shine among them like stars in the sky as you hold firmly to the word of life" (Philippians 2:14–16 NIV).

Oh, to shine and not to whine. *I desire to shine like a star and pierce the darkness, Lord. Please help me stop complaining. I want to be used by you to further your kingdom.*

God reminded me of my disgust as an unbeliever when I encountered one of his children who whined.

As a member of the Rhode Island Air National Guard, I attended combat photography school in Denver, Colorado. One of my roommates was a born-again believer. She asked to read the Bible to me. On occasion I let her, but I didn't understand it. I searched for the way to heaven and desperately wanted to comprehend Scripture. On more than one occasion, my roommate criticized the people in school and proceeded to grumble about life in general. My desire to hear the Word was snuffed out by her constant complaining. Her whining dimmed her light.

As I stared into my coffee cup, I cringed as I thought about the roommate I had three years ago. *Have I hindered others as she hindered me? Do I complain too much?* That memory lit a fire of commitment in my soul. *Stop whining, Cherrilynn, and shine like a star so others can know Jesus and find freedom. Now get to work and study the word "attitude."*

I wrote the acrostic STAR vertically on my notebook and prayed. I love acrostics. I use them often when I teach because the outline is easy to remember. After a few hours of study, the STAR principle was created.

S: see yourself as God sees you. Some of us struggle with our identity. We think we are too fat, too skinny, too ugly, or too _____ (fill in the blank). We believe we cannot please God no matter what we do. We compare ourselves with the girls in magazines or with the women's ministry leader in the church. To get the surprising truth of our real identity in Christ, we need to look at our spiritual position before salvation and after salvation.

T: transform your mind with the Word. Real transformation takes place when we allow the living and active Word of God to transform our lives. The catalyst for change is memorizing Scripture. We will learn the importance of the Word and how to remember it. Thus, we will have an arsenal of weapons for spiritual battles.

A: always pray. Prayer is talking to God. In this section, we will take a journalistic approach to prayer, dissect a prayer that will dramatically change us from the inside—the surgical prayer— and we will become equipped to fight daily spiritual battles by learning to don the armor of God through prayer.

R: refined to shine. Pain is inevitable. We must expect trials and heartache because we live in a world filled with sin and its effects. How does God use the sin of the world for his glory? The final portion of this book will address the reality of trials and tribulations and how to get through them with joy.

Over the last twenty-five years of speaking and ministering to women, I found these four principles are essential for our light to shine. We all have hearts that desire to serve God, but our brilliance can be extinguished by life's circumstances or wrong thinking. We obtain STAR quality when our light shines bright amidst the darkness, pain, and trials. To achieve this, we must apply the STAR principle, a biblical guideline to illuminate the dark areas that keep us from being a lighthouse to the world.

Shine, Don't Whine outlines each of these principles to help us walk out our journey in faith, strength, and hope. When we apply the STAR principle, our attitude begins to change. It doesn't happen overnight. It's a daily decision to believe God's Word, memorize it, and apply it. The Spirit in us works with the Word to perform, what I call, "spiritual surgery." God is the Great Physician. Scripture is his scalpel used to eradicate sin—if we remain on the operating table. Often we squirm or bolt, leaving the tumor of sin unremoved. Yes, there will be pain. We must allow faith to be our anesthesia, knowing that the lover of our soul is the only one qualified for such delicate surgery.

The result is freedom from worry, self-pity, and self-hatred. God desires to shine a spotlight into our hearts, reveal our sin, remove it, and fill the void with the truth. The Spirit is always searching for destructive thought patterns, disobedience, and hurts. We must always be ready for spiritual surgery.

Sin will continue to invade; trials will come; and pain is inevitable. We may doubt our identity in Christ, forget to meditate on the Word, allow prayer to elude us, and falter when trials come. The surgeon is always ready to remove the darkness and replace it with his light of truth. We need only ask him to reveal which principle we need to work on so that our light is not dimmed or extinguished.

I try to follow these principles daily, and God continues to take away my need to be perfect. I rarely desire to be at the center of worldly attention, but pride and the need for accolades still slither into my heart.

One Sunday morning, my pastor asked me to announce a new radio program he would host. A few pastors from different Christian denominations sponsored this program to focus on Jesus and unite the local churches. I spoke clearly and to the point. After all, I was a professional radio announcer. After church, my friend Lisa said, "Great announcement. Now I know why you work in radio." A few others also filled my pride balloon with the helium of praise. I floated toward the door.

Then a woman I had never seen before stepped into my personal space, brow furrowed. "You don't know what you're talking about. Churches are united in this area. You should be careful what you say. You will cause dissension."

Pop! My pride balloon burst. The Holy Spirit held my tongue. Years of memorizing "[B]e quick to listen, slow to speak and slow to become angry" (James 1:19 NIV) saved me embarrassment. I could only say, "Thank you. I will pray about that."

I wanted to say, "Didn't you hear the brilliant announcement? You got all the facts wrong. Listen, lady, instead of being judgmental."

The entire ride home I dissected my announcement. What did I say to make her upset?

I try to learn from every situation.

As I prayed, the Spirit impressed upon my heart. *It's not what you said; it's how you said it.*

The message I delivered was a serious message of reconciliation. I gave it with joy and spunk. I wanted people to see me more than they heard the heartbeat of the new radio program. I repented of my pride and critical attitude toward the woman, who I never saw again. I thanked God for using her to show me my flaws. Now, I pray and check my motive at the door before I speak, write, or minister. I praise God that he is still working in me.

To desire pure motives in all we think, do, and say doesn't make pure motives happen. A lifelong commitment of memorizing the Word and prayer will change our hearts, thereby changing our motives. We must compare our feelings to the Word of God and allow the Spirit to perform spiritual surgery on our sin. I will discuss more about spiritual surgery in a future chapter.

Our journey through the STAR principle will be difficult, and at times we might want to give up. We can ask God to shine the light of his Word into our heart to show us which principle applies when we find the ability to shine weakened by pride, lack of contentment, or eagerness to complain. Let's ask, "Do I see myself as God sees me? Am I not applying Scripture to my situation? When was the last time I spoke to my Father? Am I allowing the trials of this world to paralyze me?" The Spirit never fails to lovingly reveal sin, reminding us that our destination is not perfection, our destiny is Jesus—the perfect one.

* * *

For fun, I researched star classifications. I wanted to learn about the heavenly stars. After all, God created them, and his Word states we will shine like stars in the universe.

- Stars are given classifications according to their surface temperature and brightness. The O stars are the hottest, M stars the coolest.
- O stars are rare but bright.
- M stars are numerous but dim.
- Our sun's classification is somewhere in the middle.[1]

I took the liberty and used these classifications to compare and label them as Christian stars.

Since O is the hottest and most rare, I classified it as "obedient." Complete obedience is rare. Oh, to always be obedient to the Master, a bright light to lead many to righteousness. "And those who are wise shall shine like the brightness of the sky above; and those who turn many to righteousness, like the stars forever and ever" (Daniel 12:3).

---

1 . "The Classification of Stars," Atlas of the Universe, accessed June 10, 2017, http://www.atlasoftheuniverse.com/startype.html.

The more numerous yet weaker stars are "mediocre." No one wants to be mediocre with low quality, value, ability, or performance. Notice the word "mediocre" begins with "me." When life is me-focused, our light disappears into a black hole, and we are not fulfilling the purpose we were created for—to shine and point people to Jesus. God warns us about half-hearted service.

God despises mediocrity. "So, because you are lukewarm, and neither hot nor cold, I will spit you out of my mouth" (Revelation 3:16). I don't want to leave a bad taste in the mouth of my Lord, do you? An attitude of "good enough" will give us feelings of guilt. When it comes to serving God, don't we want to serve with wholehearted devotion and a willing mind, giving our best because he gave his best for us?

May our separate journeys enable us to shine for the Lord. May our light lead others to the lover of their souls, like the star that guided wise men to Jesus.

We must take the time to understand the lessons the Word of God has for us. I sometimes fall into the I-have-studied-this-and-know-it trap. How prideful of me. Scripture states we should be reminded of what we have already learned. The apostle Paul writes to the church at Rome, "I have written you quite boldly on some points to remind you of them again, because of the grace God gave me" (Romans 15:15 NIV).

God chose the right moment to reveal a life-altering truth to me. The light of Scripture permeated a place so dark, I was scared to acknowledge it existed. God knew the depths of pain lurking in my soul waiting to ambush me again. As a good Father, he knew I was ready to face the hideous lies that haunted me.

I read the book of John five or six times as a new believer. I memorized John 1:12 so I would be equipped to give the salvation message. One day, I taught another new believer where to find this verse in the Bible. I had her read the verse. As she read, she included v. 13, "[C]hildren born not of natural descent, nor of human decision or a husband's will, but born of God."

"Read that again, please," I said. As she read it, I bit my tongue as I held back tears. *Can it be? Am I here because God wants me here and not because of my abusive father?* The invisible wall I placed around my heart began to disintegrate with the light of God's love and the truth of his Word. My silent prayer for God to show me my worth in him was answered at a time I least expected. Imagine if I shut my ears off because I had already heard these verses. The chains would have remained longer. I'm forever grateful. I now show this verse to others who have endured abuse from parents or have difficulties seeing themselves as God sees them.

Star quality begins when we memorize and obey God's word. His Word is living and active. When we consume the Word and make it a part of us, surgery commences, and our attitude will change. "For the word of God is alive and active. Sharper than any double-edged sword, it penetrates even to dividing soul and spirit, joints and marrow; it judges the thoughts and attitudes of the heart" (Hebrews 4:12 NIV).

The Word can give us the feeling of a warm hug. Scripture can encourage us, direct us, and maybe provide a gentle spiritual smack in the head when needed. I've had plenty of the attitude-adjusting slaps. Only the Word of God works in harmony with the Holy Spirit to change each of us. The more verses we know, the brighter our light. Let's go learn to shine!

=============================

Memory verse
Philippians 2:14–16 NIV, "Do everything without grumbling or arguing, so that you may become blameless and pure, 'children of God without fault in a warped and crooked generation.' Then you will shine among them like stars."

Light reflection questions:

1. What classification of STAR are you? Explain.

2. What causes discontentment in your life? Why?

3. Is there an attitude that needs adjusting in your life? Explain.

S: See Yourself as God Sees You

"Even as he (God) chose us in him (Jesus) before
the foundation of the world, that we should be
holy and blameless before him" (Ephesians 1:4).

Before Salvation

"I bet you can't sing!" declared a voice from the back of the classroom.

"No, she is too ugly to sing," another boy said as he laughed with the rest of the students.

Fifth grade was brutal. The kids shunned and made fun of me for being poor. I didn't wear the latest fashion. I had three outfits that I mixed and matched, and the class took note. I felt like a bug under a microscope—dead inside and ready to be dissected at any moment.

One afternoon, my classmates heckled me into auditioning for the part of Nancy in our school play, *Oliver Twist*.

"She's chicken!" said Sue.

Janice had finished her beautiful rendition of "Where Is Love?" Everyone knew Janice had the best voice in the class. I wanted to be accepted. My stomach did flip-flops as I walked to the piano and waited for the music.

The class snickered.

"She's a fool. She can't sing. She's ugly."

"Didn't she wear that horrible shirt Monday?"

I wanted to cry and flee the room. The piano played; I opened my mouth and sang. Laughter turned into shock. Janice looked mad. The music teacher looked pleased. And the boys looked at their shoes. I got the part of Nancy in our class play.

On opening night, I could see my mom and stepdad in the audience. The lights were bright, and I was in heaven. I loved the spotlight on me. I sang the song flawlessly and received congratulations and hugs from parents and friends.

Janice and Sue, the most popular girls in the class, acknowledged my existence with, "Great job, Cherrilynn." I basked in my newfound fame.

Only a few weeks after the curtain closed, my classmates forgot about the play and me. My heart broke. My friends only liked me because I could sing. The irony is I can't sing well anymore. I had to identify myself in another way.

* * *

God's truth can permeate the heart no matter how we describe ourselves. My sisters and I are living proof there is hope for all. The three of us reacted to our father's abuse differently. My younger sister withdrew from everyone; shyness was her mask. My older sister became rebellious—she left home at sixteen years of age, the aftermath of years of torture.

Me? I was a hurting child in need of an outlet. I mirrored my father. I took my anger out on my younger sister. I threw her to the ground, broke her glasses, and belittled her. Though I still cry from time to time when I think of the pain I inflicted on my sister, I rejoice that God wasn't content to leave us there. Each of us no longer identifies ourselves by the brokenness. We claim we are children of God and best friends.

What do you see when you look in the mirror? Do you see what God sees? Do you complain about your outward appearance or character traits? Do you compare yourself with others? What you see may not be a reality. When I looked in the mirror, my mind would not allow my reality to reflect the truth. I saw myself as ugly, stupid, and hopeless one day, then fun, smart, and pretty on another day. The reflection changed with my moods or someone's comments.

I had an unbalanced and sometimes unrealistic view of myself. At times, I thought too highly of myself. *Look at you! You got the leadership award. They don't give those out to just anyone.* Or, *I must be cute! The most popular guy in class looked my way.*

Other times, I magnified my imperfections. *That guy's not looking at you; he is looking at the zit on your nose. You're a failure. Even your dad hates you. Why are you alive?*

I had to get off the emotional roller coaster caused by situational self-talk and stop judging myself in light of my circumstances and emotions. The fit of my jeans or the flawlessness of my skin shouldn't determine my worth. I needed stability. I needed direction. I needed the truth.

Do you ever feel as if you're on a roller coaster of acceptance and criticism, not knowing what each turn holds? How do we get off this ride of uncertainty and get our feet firmly planted on the ground? The ground we call truth.

There is hope, and it's not found in a smaller jean size or a clear complexion. It's realized in Jesus. He is steadfast, unmovable, and trustworthy. He is the truth. He will stop the ride of emotional uncertainty.

David, the giant slayer, was a strong but humble shepherd who became God's choice to replace Saul as king of Israel. He entrusted his soul and body to God, even with King Saul and his army in pursuit to kill him. During his times of distress, David knew God would not lead him astray. "For you are my rock and my fortress; and for your name's sake you lead me and guide me" (Psalm 31:3).

David knew God would be there to guide him to the truth. We can have that same confidence. So, how do we exit this emotional roller coaster?

God's view of us is critical for stability. Biblical knowledge of our status in God's eyes before and after salvation helps us obtain the complete truth concerning our identity. We grasp the deep importance of what Jesus accomplished on the cross when we see our desperate, isolated state before salvation and compare it with the righteousness we have in Christ, after salvation. The bridge from darkness to light is salvation through the blood of Christ.

The "before" picture is wretched. Only a divine intervention by God can rescue us from this pathetic situation.

* * *

I have a vivid imagination. One day I tried to describe my life before Jesus. I knew I felt dead. Ephesians 2:1–2 convinced me of my useless existence, "And you were dead in the trespasses and sins in which you once walked, following the course of this world." I thought of the zombies on television who wandered through life with no purpose or meaning. That was me. An enemy of God without consciousness of the Holy One. I walked in darkness, oblivious to why God created me. I lived among the other spiritually dead—those who do what is right in their own eyes, trying to please themselves and not the one whose image they bear. What an awful way to exist.

Life was scary with no hope; my heart forever flatlined. *Does everyone have this experience?* I needed resuscitation. The Word of God along with the Holy Spirit were the vital shock paddles to bring me to life.

The saying "truth hurts" is an understatement. When I studied the fate of humanity apart from Jesus, I wept. I was God's enemy deserving death—eternal separation from my Creator. I did not want to be an enemy of God. I thought I had something to offer him. How did I, along with all humans, inherit this death?

To understand how this happened, we must go to the beginning. If you know this, please stick with me. The more we solidify the truth in our hearts, the stronger our witness and faith.

"Then God said, 'Let us make man in our image, after our likeness,' . . . So God created man in his own image, in the image of God he created him; male and female he created them" (Genesis 1:26–27). Adam and Eve were created in the image of God and had a perfect relationship with him. They walked through the Garden of Eden enjoying the fragrant aroma of the flowers, playing with the animals, and eating whatever they wanted, except the fruit from the Tree of the Knowledge of Good and Evil, as God commanded.

These two children of God had total dependency and trust in God. Imagine being able to walk with God without shame or guilt. Adam and Eve truly lived in paradise until the serpent deceived them with lies. Adam and Eve disobeyed their Creator and partook of the fruit from the only forbidden tree. I encourage you to reread the story found in Genesis 3.

When my son was young, he'd make a bad decision or blatantly sin by lying to me. He'd say, "Oh, Adam and Eve, why did you have to eat the fruit? Now I'm in trouble because of you." He was too young to understand that given the same opportunity, he would choose the forbidden fruit too. We are all in trouble due to disobedience.

Because of their defiance, God had to ban them from the Garden of Eden. No more walks with God, no more shameless days basking in the sun. God had to protect them from their bad choice. He had to cast them out of the garden to prevent them from eating from the Tree of Life. So, what does the Tree of Life have to do with them getting kicked out of paradise?

Then the LORD God said, "Behold, the man has become like one of us in knowing good and evil. Now, lest he reach out his hand and take also of the tree of life and eat, and live forever—"therefore the LORD God sent him out from the garden to work the ground from which he was taken. (Genesis 3:22–23)

What would happen if they had been allowed to stay? Would they have eaten from that tree? We don't know, but God knew. If Adam and Eve ate from the Tree of Life after they ate from the Tree of the Knowledge of Good and Evil, they would have lived forever in a state of sin. There would be no hope of reconciliation with their Creator. God in his mercy and grace chased Adam and Eve from the garden and guided them to a safe place. A place of hope.

Now mankind is separated from God. A pitiful state of affairs. "Therefore, just as sin came into the world through one man, and death through sin, and so death spread to all men because all sinned" (Romans 5:12).

I thought to myself, *If it were me, I would never have done that. It's not fair to condemn all humanity for something Adam and Eve did more than four thousand years ago.*

I had to be honest with myself when I thought it through. I'd be tempted by the serpent and eat the fruit.

Through Scripture, we know we are all born into sin. I don't like this fact, but I cannot argue with God.

Watch babies. They're cute and cuddly, but they're little sinners. Rebellion is built into their bones. Watch toddlers. They throw hissy fits, scream, and yell to get what they want. We call it the terrible twos, but it will last forever if unaided by the intervention and discipline of God's truth, grace, and mercy. This truth may make us uncomfortable, but it is still the truth.

Shontell, a great woman of God and a true friend, taught my son his first word—flower. The word sounded more like "phhower," as he pointed to the fake flowers in the church nursery.

Shontell loves children, and the Word of God is foremost in her life. The first time she met Michael she said, "Hello, you little sinner!" At first, I felt offended by her comment, but I quickly realized that she's right.

The dilemma for you and me is how do we reconcile our relationship with God? The bad news: We don't. We can't. Scripture is the only reliable source for answers, so let's continue the journey. I promise better news is ahead.

"When Adam had lived 130 years, he fathered a son in his own likeness, after his image, and named him Seth" (Genesis 5:3).

Seth was in Adam's fallen image and likeness, and we are too. Even though man was originally created in the image of God, sin corrupts us. We're all sons and daughters of Adam, born with a sin nature and separated from God.

The concept of being separated from my Creator scared me. I could not fix the problem, but God, in his perfect love and mercy, provided a solution—Jesus—who chose to enter this imperfect world. Our Savior exchanged angelic praise for rebellious taunts. He was sinless. Jesus willingly went to the cross for us. He said this about the cross, "I lay down my life that I may take it up again. No one takes it from me, but I lay it down of my own accord" (John 10:17–18).

His mission is reconciliation. He knew our desperate condition and chose to sacrifice himself—a perfect, sinless offering. Jesus never complained about his mission. He never whined to the Father.

Jesus understands our dilemma and temptation. "For we do not have a high priest who is unable to sympathize with our weaknesses, but one who in every respect has been tempted as we are, yet without sin" (Hebrews 4:15).

Like many others, my son acknowledged his futile state before God, repented, and now has a vibrant relationship with Jesus. He no longer blames Adam and Eve when he chooses to sin. Michael owns his decision to sin and asks for forgiveness, stating his sin against the person and God. He prays and asks God to help him in that area of sin.

Now that we have looked at the bad news let's continue our journey.

The process of freedom in Christ won't make sense without the help of the Holy Spirit. The Spirit is the divine teacher who God gives to us at salvation. If the Lord is calling you, today is the day of redemption. Do not wait. Have you experienced a tug on your heart? Don't delay. Your Creator beckons you to come!

The plan of salvation is found in the back of the book, "Shine for Salvation." I encourage you to read that chapter before you continue the journey. Salvation is as simple as A, B, C.

A: acknowledge you're a sinner.
B: believe Jesus is God and that he died on the cross for your sin.
C: confess your sin and cry out in repentance.

The darkest part of the journey is over. The news gets better. In the next chapter, we won't have any reason to complain when we see ourselves as God sees us.

More truth awaits. Are you ready?

===========================

Memory verse
Colossians 1:21, "And you, who once were alienated and hostile in mind, doing evil deeds."

Light reflection questions:

1. Why is a nonbeliever an enemy of God? Explain.

2. What can we do to earn salvation? Explain.

3. Are babies born sinless? Explain.

After Salvation

Chills went down my spine the first time I heard the voice of God in the movie, *The Ten Commandments*: "Put off thy shoes from off thy feet, for the place whereon thou standest is holy ground."

My five-year-old brain truly thought it was God.

I wanted to take my shoes off and obey, even if our household was far from serving God.

Twenty-two years later, God saved my miserable soul.

I still get the chills when I see Moses bow down to God and take off his sandals. Now I know he was another sinner just like me, but I still long to stand on holy ground with God.

When I was a new believer, I looked forward to singing. At the age of twenty-eight, I found myself listening to Christian music instead of rock and roll.

My favorite hymn— "Holy Ground."

One Sunday morning, as the congregation sang, "We are standing on holy ground," the Spirit convicted my heart. *If you believe this, why do you go out to clubs and dance while the guys ogle you?*

Ouch! Was that God speaking to me?

The previous night, my sister and I went to a dance club with friends. I loved to dance. In fact, I won contests for limbo, twist, and free dancing. *What's wrong with dancing?*

We considered leaving early after a guy said something rude and provocative about my dancing. My sister and I felt a twinge of conviction, but did not act on it.

The next day, as I finished singing the song, conviction and sorrow overwhelmed me. I repented immediately.

I realized it wasn't the dancing that displeased God (King David danced); it was the way I danced. It incited men to stumble. If I truly admit it, I wanted the attention. I felt guilty and needed a reminder of God's love and my identity in Christ.

The Word states, "Even as he (God) chose us in him (Jesus) before the foundation of the world, that we should be holy and blameless before him. In love, he predestined us for adoption as sons through Jesus Christ, according to the purpose of his will" (Ephesians 1:4–5).

We were chosen before the foundation of the world even when God knew our debauchery. That means we have nothing to do with our salvation. We cannot earn it, and we cannot do anything to lose it, like dancing. We are redeemed and saved by the grace of God.

In him we have redemption through his blood, the forgiveness of our trespasses, according to the riches of his grace." (Ephesians 1:7)

But God, being rich in mercy, because of the great love with which he loved us, even when we were dead in our trespasses, made us alive together with Christ—by grace you have been saved. (Ephesians 2:4–5)

"Grace" means "unmerited favor." Grace is not getting the punishment we deserve for our sin. Now that's something to dance about.

"[God] who saved us and called us to a holy calling, not because of our works but because of his own purpose and grace, which he gave us in Christ Jesus before the ages began" (2 Timothy 1:9).

The good news gets better. Did you know, as a child of God, you are a gift to Jesus from God? "I have manifested your name to the people whom you gave me out of the world. Yours they were, and you gave them to me, and they have kept your word" (John 17:6).

So when someone says to you, "You think you're God's gift," you can reply, "I know I am!"

We are not a gift that sits on a shelf. We are saved for a purpose. "For we are his workmanship, created in Christ Jesus for good works, which God prepared beforehand, that we should walk in them" (Ephesians 2:10).

The king of the universe uses us to further his kingdom. He equips us to be his ambassadors. We are saved to serve as Jesus came to serve. We belong to Christ now. "You are not your own, for you were bought with a price. So glorify God in your body" (1 Corinthians 6:19b–20).

Our view of self may hinder us from being used by God.

I struggled with this biblical truth as a new believer. I could not shake the guilt and shame of past sin, so I memorized Ephesians 1:4–5 along with Psalm 139:16b, "[I]n your book were written, every one of them, the days that were formed for me, when as yet there was none of them."

I would say to myself, *If God chose me before the foundations of the world knowing my depravity, I can't earn my salvation or lose it. He loves me just the way I am.*

The change was slow. In fact, I did not believe it for the first few years.

However, the Word proved to be living and active. Scripture began transforming me from the inside out and performed what I like to call "spiritual surgery." The Word removed the cancer of sin and replaced it with the healing truth. I now see myself as God sees me. I'm released from the chains of perfection. When I struggle with my identity, I refer to the STAR principle. I am compelled to teach it to others.

While driving to a speaking engagement, I practiced my teaching for that day. The topic happened to be this section of

Shine, Don't Whine. I bet I looked crazy to other drivers as I talked to myself and waved my hand around. I still had a hand on the steering wheel. I recited this Bible verse, "I give them eternal life, and they will never perish, and no one will snatch them out of my hand" (John 10:28).

I shivered as God gave me an image in my head. Tears bounced off the goosebumps on my arm. What a glorious picture. I wanted to throw my hands up in praise and adoration to my King. Of course, I resisted so I would make it to my destination safely.

As I held out my hand and made a fist, I pictured my hand as the loving hand of Christ (minus the nail polish). The Holy Spirit reminded me that we are in the palm of his hand, safe and secure. The lesson did not stop there; the Spirit revealed even more.

When God looks at Christ's hand, he does not see us. He sees the hand of the Son he loves. He also sees the scar left from the nail piercing. The reminder that his innocent Son endured the most intense physical, emotional, and spiritual pain. I remembered the words that Christ cried from the cross. The words that echoed throughout heaven and now in my heart. "It is finished!"

I almost crashed the car, but I made it to my destination to share this beautiful, poignant word picture. There were tears and ah-ha moments.

Our identity is in Christ. This truth is vital to believers. We have passed from death to life.

The apostle Paul, originally called Saul, was a well-educated Jew. He was overzealous for the law, which led him to hunt Christians and have them stoned to death. After his conversion, (Acts 9:1–19) he still claimed to be the vilest of sinners, but he knew his identity was in Christ.

"I have been crucified with Christ. It is no longer I who live, but Christ who lives in me. And the life I now live in the flesh I live by faith in the Son of God, who loved me and gave himself for me" (Galatians 2:20).

Paul wrote most of the New Testament. He endured beatings, imprisonment, and shipwrecks because he wanted to proclaim the salvation of the one who saved him from the bondage of performing works to obtain God's favor. Paul died a martyr. Based on historical events of the day, it is likely that Paul was beheaded.

* * *

Before we embark on the next chapter, I must tell you a story that gave me the chills or "Holy Ghost goosebumps." I first heard this story on Christian radio. I'm changing the names because I do not remember the original names of the couple. The analogy and application of the story are what we're after.

There was a woman named Martha and a man named Kevin who got married right out of high school. Martha loved anything to do with Buckingham Palace. She and Kevin had children. Martha would always speak of her desire to go to see the Changing of the Guards at Buckingham Palace. For their fiftieth wedding anniversary, the children purchased an all-expenses paid trip to England to see the Changing of the Guards. Martha was so excited; she rattled off all the facts she knew. The big day finally arrived. Martha's dream had finally come true. As they were sitting in their hotel room overlooking the gardens at Buckingham Palace, Kevin sat glancing out the window onto the courtyard. Martha was combing her hair getting ready for the long-awaited day.

"Martha, is today a special day?"

"Of course, it is our fiftieth anniversary, silly!" Martha blushed.

Kevin kept gazing out the window with a puzzled look on his face.

"Martha, you must look, the guards are wearing white!"

Martha gasped and placed her brush on the dresser. She hurried over to the window.

"This cannot be. The Queen ordained them to wear red. Something's not right."

Martha furrowed her brow as she and Kevin investigated the window. They realized they were looking at the red coats through the red-tinted glass.

"It makes the red coats look white!" Martha exclaimed.

What is the color of sin? "Come now, let us reason together, says the Lord: though your sins are like scarlet [red], they shall be as white as snow; though they are red like crimson, they shall become like wool" (Isaiah 1:18).

The Bible states that sin is red.

What color is the blood of Christ? Jesus is human, so we know it is red. When God looks at our red sin through the red blood of Jesus, he sees white!

I want to jump for joy or dance the jig when I think about this analogy. We are made righteous by the blood of Christ.

Blessed be the God and Father of our Lord Jesus Christ, who has blessed us in Christ with every spiritual blessing in the heavenly places, even as he chose us in him before the foundation of the world, that we should be holy and blameless before him. In love he predestined us for adoption as sons through Jesus Christ, according to the purpose of his will, to the praise of his glorious grace, with which he has blessed us in the Beloved. (Ephesians 1:3–6)

We are in Christ now. The words, "in Christ," appear eighty-seven times in the ESV translation of the Bible. Remember the visual of being in Christ's hand? We are loved, protected, and cherished. We have no reason to whine. Let's shine!

=============================

Memory verse
1 Corinthians 6:19b–20, "You are not your own, for you were bought with a price. So glorify God in your body."

Light reflection questions.

1. How does God see his children? Explain.

2. What does it mean to be in Christ's hand?

3. Who gives us the power for change? Explain.

Saved to Serve

Does the word "servant" really mean "slave?" I whispered to myself in disbelief.

As a speaker/teacher, I pray about each event. I was so excited to speak at the church where I obtained my firm Bible foundation. I wanted to share and give back to the women who invested valuable time in me.

God gave me a remarkable gift, the time to study Scripture and take Bible courses. I cherish this treasure. I chose to teach a study on biblical servanthood. After all, I sign my correspondence "Saved to Serve." It's time to really learn it and live it more. I began my study by researching the word "servant." I had to carefully read and reread the online concordance, and I checked many verses and found the original word "slave" was translated to "servant." This made my skin crawl and the hair on the back of my neck stand on end.

How could this be, Lord? Thoughts of the horrific treatment of slaves in America and elsewhere ran through my mind. As I continued my study, God showed me the true meaning of biblical slavery. It may not be what you think. I am not a theologian. I cherish the truth of the Word of God and make every effort to handle it correctly. This chapter only touches on some of the basic points. Please do a more in-depth study of this word on your own. You will be blessed.

The Greek word for "servant" is *doulos*, and it is used many times in the New Testament. It's never interchanged with the word "servant" in the Greek. There are about five other words in the bible that mean "to serve," but *doulos* is not one of them.

Slaves were common during the Old Testament and New Testament times. There were laws concerning the treatment of slaves.

Leviticus 25:43 says, "You shall not rule over him ruthlessly but shall fear your God."

Deuteronomy 15:12–14 says, "If your brother, a Hebrew man or a Hebrew woman, is sold to you, he shall serve you six years, and in the seventh year you shall let him go free from you. And when you let him go free from you, you shall not let him go empty-handed. You shall furnish him liberally out of your flock, out of your threshing floor, and out of your winepress. As the LORD your God has blessed you, you shall give to him."

Now that is a different picture than I imagined. Slaves were treated with respect and kindness. Kidnapping someone and selling them into slavery was forbidden by God. "If a man is found stealing one of his brothers of the people of Israel, and if he treats him as a slave or sells him, then that thief shall die. So you shall purge the evil from your midst" (Deuteronomy 24:7).

In the New Testament, Jesus did not free the slaves, and the apostle Paul gave these instructions:

Let each one remain in the same calling in which he was called. Were you called while a slave [doulos]? Do not be concerned about it; but if you can be made free, rather use it. For he who is called in the Lord while a slave [doulos] is the Lord's freedman. Likewise he who is called while free is Christ's slave [doulos]. You were bought at a price; do not become slaves of men. Brothers and sisters, each person, as responsible to God, should remain in the situation they were in when God called them. (1 Corinthians 7:20–24)

Peter understood this also.

Servants [doulos], be submissive to your masters with all fear, not only to the good and gentle, but also to the harsh. God is over the master and he will deal with them if they are abusive. (1 Peter 2:18)

So why are we learning about servant/slaves? Now that we have the real picture of what God means by slave, we should not be alarmed when God calls us to be like Jesus—the ultimate slave/servant.

Have this mind among yourselves, which is yours in Christ Jesus, who, though he was in the form of God, did not count equality with God a thing to be grasped, but emptied himself, by taking the form of a servant [doulos], being born in the likeness of men. And being found in human form, he humbled himself by becoming obedient to the point of death, even death on a cross. (Philippians 2:5–8)

We are to think like a slave and learn how to serve like Jesus. What do we do when we don't feel like serving due to being tired, lonely, angry, or rebellious?

For sin will have no dominion over you, since you are not under law but under grace. What then? Are we to sin because we are not under law but under grace? By no means! Do you not know that if you present yourselves to anyone as obedient slaves [*doulos*], you are slaves [*doulos*] of the one whom you obey, either of sin, which leads to death, or of obedience, which leads to righteousness? But thanks be to God, that you who were once slaves [*doulos*] of sin have become obedient from the heart to the standard of teaching to which you were committed. . . . But now that you have been set free from sin and have become slaves of God. (Romans 6: 14–17, 22)

Sometimes we forget that sin has no dominion over us. We have the strength to overcome through the resurrection power of the Holy Spirit. Sin is not our master; Christ is our ruler. He redeemed us from the pit of hell and brought us into his perfect light. "You were bought at a price. Therefore honor God with your bodies" (1 Corinthians 6:20).

God loves us so much that we should desire to serve him. There was a time where I said, "Nobody owns me!" I lived in fear and built walls so I would not be hurt again. When God desired to show his love toward me, I was hesitant.

How can God love me when my own earthly father did not? I began to pray for God to take the fear away.

The Spirit you received does not make you slaves [*doulos*] so that you live in fear again; rather, the Spirit you received brought about your adoption to sonship. And by him we cry, "Abba, Father." (Romans 8:15)

Here are two other verses that ignited my desire to serve.

There is no fear in love. But perfect love drives out fear, because fear has to do with punishment. The one who fears is not made perfect in love. (1 John 4:18)

In fact, this is love for God: to keep his commands. And his commands are not burdensome. (1 John 5:5)

I desired to serve my Master and be obedient. He did not want to punish me; Christ died for my sin and now sees me as righteous.

One evening, I asked God to reveal his ultimate purpose for my life. He gave me a picture in my head. Have you seen those red plastic baskets restaurants use to serve fries, chips, and chicken wings? God showed me a basket as I begged to him use me. The vision in my head was clear.

The basket had some pita bread broken into pieces. The Spirit impressed upon my heart as I prayed. *You are the basket. You will serve me; be prepared. Now go to the Bible and study both stories on Jesus feeding the multitudes.*

That night I read Matthew 14:10–21—the story of Jesus feeding the five thousand. This miracle took place after the beheading of John the Baptist. Jesus was heartbroken. He tried to go to a desolate place, but he was followed by people who wanted to be healed. He had compassion on them; he healed them and fed them.

Again, in Matthew 15:29–39, Jesus was on a mountain healing many. He was joyful, and the people glorified the God of Israel because of all the miracles. Then Jesus fed four thousand.

I prayed and compared these two stories. The Spirit echoed in my heart, *Like Jesus, you will feed many, whether you are in physical or emotional pain, in a desolate place, or on a mountaintop. No matter the circumstance, you are my servant. I will use you when I want and how I want. Be prepared to shine your light.*

I thought of the red plastic basket in my vision. It has no great value, but it held the bread, the sustenance of life.

We hold the Word of God in our head and heart, which can nourish others. The power of the Spirit at work in and through us can bring healing, conviction, joy, encouragement, and truth to the multitudes. God will test us as his servant.

There have been times I was so weak and tired, but he called me to minister. I did not want to, but he reminded me of the basket. I was obedient, and God was glorified.

No matter when or where we serve, our Savior reminds us that serving in his power will reap rewards.

Remember when Jesus fed the multitude? There were leftovers.

Jesus served when he was tired, lonely, misunderstood, and filled with joy. He served to the point of death. He had victory, his service reaped eternal rewards, and we are part of that reward. Because of this, we are called to obedience by serving. We are to be like Jesus.

For those whom he foreknew he also predestined to be conformed to the image of his Son. (Romans 8:29)

At times, I fail at being a servant; my light dims, so I turn to the STAR principles to see which one has blown a fuse. I recharge with the truth and my light brightens.

I find great joy as a conduit used by our great God to change someone's life. There's no experience like it.

Will you join me and seek to serve our Abba no matter what he calls us to do? Commit to shine and not whine as we fulfill the Great Commandment—to love the Lord our God with all our heart, soul, mind, and strength, and to love others as ourselves.

God is love. His love never fails. Love keeps his stars bright.

Love enables us to accept our identity in Christ.

* * *

Congratulations! We have journeyed through the first portion of the STAR principle. As we continue through the other three principles, we must always remember each one is vital to our shineability.

If we begin to complain and our light dims due to the lies of negative self-image, we must take hold of this principle. I don't like the word "self" when describing identity or usefulness. Our image and worth come from God's viewpoint, not from humans' viewpoints. He is the king of the universe. We belong to him and serve him. He purchased us with the blood of his precious Son. So, God sees us as righteous and loveable; we must accept the truth and live in it.

I no longer see myself as an unwanted little girl, one whose daddy left her. My Abba in heaven loves me, flaws and all. He promises never to leave, and I believe him and want to serve him. These promises are yours too. He knows we are not perfect, but we are perfectly loved.

The word of God working in our heart and mind is the catalyst to change our negative self-talk to the truth—to shine, not whine.

=============================

Memory verse
Matthew 20:28, "[E]ven as the Son of Man came not to be served but to serve, and to give his life as a ransom for many."

Light reflection questions:

1. How were slaves meant to be treated in the Bible?

2. Whose slave are you? Explain.

3. What was Jesus's attitude mentioned in Philippians 2?

T: Transformed Mind

"[Y]ou were taught with regard to your former way of life to put on your old self which is being corrupted by deceitful desires to be made new in the attitude of your minds" (Ephesians 4:22–23 NIV).

Feelings Versus Truth

Guilty feelings gripped me, choking out the truth of the Word.

Everything was my fault. At least, that's how I felt. If a friend or family member was unhappy, I blamed myself. If there were deadly tornados in the Midwest, somehow it was my fault because I didn't pray enough. If two people were whispering, it had to be about me. My thoughts hurled me in many directions. Guilt, shame, and despair quickly turned to trust, hope, and overconfidence with my circumstances. I needed freedom from this selfish mind-set. I found nothing amusing on the roller-coaster ride of guilt and lies.

Do you ever experience dizziness from riding the merry-go-round of emotions? Do you want freedom from the carnival of confusion?

Living by emotion caused chaos in my life. After I sinned against God and confessed, I still felt guilty. If my guilt truly is taken away, why does it cling to me? The verse from Isaiah 6:7 was my mantra: "Your guilt is taken away and your sin atoned for."

I knew the Word changes hearts, but my feelings of guilt remained. Was I missing something?

People would give me advice when I felt guilty, such as, "You just have to forgive yourself," my friend told me.

I sinned against God and another believer. My heart broke, and no matter how much I asked God to forgive me, I did not feel forgiven. But forgiving myself? Somehow that did not sit right in my spirit. However, I would repeat the phrase to others when they felt the lack of forgiveness.

"You just have to forgive yourself," I stated. But inside I asked, *What does this mean? Is it biblical?*

Through prayer and study, the Lord revealed to me why my spirit was unsettled about the statement. As a believer, I know sin is inevitable. Even the apostle Paul confessed his struggle: "For I do not do the good I want to do, but the evil I do not want to do is what I keep on doing" (Romans 7:19).

What did the apostle Paul do when he encountered his own sin?

What a wretched man I am! Who will rescue me from this body that is subject to death? Thanks be to God, who delivers me through Jesus Christ our Lord! (Romans 7:24–25 NIV)

He acknowledged his sin. He acknowledged the need to be rescued from it. He thanked God for Jesus's deliverance. He did not forgive himself.

As I continued to study, I heard these questions echo in my head: *Did you hang on the cross? Was the sin of the world put on you? Did you endure excruciating pain? Are you God?*

Tears filled my eyes as I exclaimed, "NO! NO! NO! NO! You did it, Lord. You were the one."

I remembered the following verses.

He himself bore our sins in his body on the cross, so that we might die to sins and live for righteousness. (1 Peter 2:24 NIV)

For there is one God and one mediator between God and mankind, the man Christ Jesus, who gave himself as a ransom for all people. (1 Timothy 2:5–6 NIV)

Jesus alone can forgive sin. We must repent, remind ourselves of his free gift of eternal life, and apply the truth of our status before God. In Christ we are righteous.

I no longer tell people to forgive themselves. I remind them of their identity in Christ and encourage them with the truth of the Word: "Let us draw near to God with a sincere heart and with the full assurance that faith brings, having our hearts sprinkled to cleanse us from a guilty conscience and having our bodies washed with pure water" (Hebrews 10:22 NIV).

There is therefore now no condemnation for those who are in Christ Jesus. (Romans 8:1)

Meanwhile, I claimed these verses for myself as I wrestled between truth and emotion. It took years to resolve why my feelings of guilt remained, even when I knew I was forgiven.

One morning, the battle became so intense and the feeling of guilt almost wrecked me as I drove to work. The emotion lingered long after the event.

I felt the warmth of the spring sun through the windshield as I sang to Christian music.

What is that flying in the sky? I asked myself. I saw a flash of light in the sky. Fear gripped my heart as I slammed on the brakes. Other cars stopped behind mine. There was something in the middle of the highway, and I almost hit it. I caught my breath, prayed, and stepped out of my car to assess the situation. To my left, about one hundred yards away, in the median, was a red Jeep on its side. In front of the Jeep was a limp body in the grass. The object that caught the morning sunlight must have been the Jeep flying through the air. I scanned to the right; about fifty yards in front of me was what looked like a bundle of clothes in the middle of three lanes of traffic.

Oh my, it's a man! I gasped under my breath. *Thank you, Lord, for making me stop.*

A month earlier, I had earned my emergency medical technician certification. I knew what to do at the scene of an accident. I had the knowledge to help these men. I expressed my dilemma. *Lord, which body do I go to first?* I cried out as I walked slowly to the scene.

I felt frightened and confused, but knew God would help me. I approached the man on the road instead of the one on the grass. His limp body looked like a rag doll as he remained motionless in the middle of the highway. Now, as an EMT, I should have immobilized the gentleman's neck to prevent injury or further damage to the spine. I did not. I did, however, observe he was unconscious and breathing. Instead, I laid my hands on him and cried out to God. The intense feeling to pray overshadowed procedure. My body shivered as I asked God to intervene. A few minutes later, I opened my tear-filled eyes to what looked like a movie scene. Many onlookers stared at me while police, fire, and ambulance crews arrived to perform their duties. I looked to my right, and to my joy and amazement, there was a man holding the neck of the patient to immobilize it. I asked this hero who he was. God sent an off-duty fireman. The police told us to leave the area. As I drove to work, I trembled and stormed the gates of heaven on behalf of the two men.

I could not concentrate at work. My supervisor listened as I told him about my terrifying morning. He encouraged me to call the police station to find out what happened to the gentlemen.

"Rhode Island State Police, how may I direct your call?"

"Yes, I would like information on the accident on RT 4 North this morning. I was the first on the scene."

"Hold on, I will put you through to the officer handling that case."

"Thank you." My body fidgeted in the chair.

"How may I help you?" the officer said.

The sound of his voice calmed me. I explained the incident. My heart beat faster and faster as I hesitated to ask the difficult question that had haunted my mind for the last two hours.

"Officer, what happened to the man in the middle of the road?"

It seemed like forever before I heard his answer.

"He is going to make it!"

"YES! Thank you, LORD!"

I was overjoyed and, for a moment, forgot I was sitting behind a desk in a medical clinic. My joyful declaration startled a few of the patients in the waiting room.

I held my breath as I asked the next question.

"How about the man in the median?"

"He died at the scene."

My heart broke, and I burst into tears. I thanked the officer and hung up the phone.

Lord, you asked me to go to the man on the road. Why? If I went to the man in the median, maybe he would have survived too! Did I hear you right?

The gloom of guilt for not going to the man in the median chased me and tried to rob me of my peace. I questioned if I really heard God. I quoted my two verses, "[N]o condemnation . . . guilt is taken away . . ." Would I ever find relief?

My angst over the situation decreased over time. I knew I wasn't in sin going to the man in the road. I knew I heard God correctly. However, the feeling of guilt remained with the pain.

The fight between my feelings and the truth came to an end one morning as I sat in the pew of my Church. Our family had moved from Rhode Island to New Hampshire to take care of my Aunt Marion. Life was arduous. The effects of my chronic illness, my husband out of work, and my son having difficulties in school occupied my mind.

Added to that, I felt guilty because my son wanted to visit a friend in the next town after church, and we could not afford the gas because I mismanaged our money and purchased a blouse.

Lord, if we are justified and not condemned, why do I still feel guilty after I confess?

My ears perked when the pastor said, "Sin leaves a spiritual wound that needs to heal. You are not being condemned."

Did the pastor read my mind? Did he know what tormented me? Did he dive deep in my inner thoughts?

The pastor repeated himself, "When we sin against God, we have a spiritual wound that needs to heal. The feeling is the healing process."

I repeated to myself, *The feeling is the healing! Healing takes time. It's not guilt. Hallelujah!*

If the congregation could hear into the spiritual realm, they would have heard my chains of guilt hit the wood floor under my pew.

I was free. The wrestling was over. God was not condemning me. I knew it in my head, and now I had an explanation for the feelings that lingered. I wanted to do cartwheels in the aisle, but you don't do gymnastics in a Baptist church.

The feeling is the healing! I whispered again.

Our enemy wants us chained to feelings of guilt. He schemes to immobilize us with lies.

I still struggle with emotions. My friends have shared the same struggle. How do we jump off this ride bound for continual confusion and condemnation and stand on the solid ground of right thinking? How do we stop comparing ourselves to others or condemning ourselves? The Word of God has the answer.

We determined through Scripture that mankind stands guilty of sin before God. Through the death of Christ, we are no longer guilty. We are justified. "Therefore, as one trespass led to condemnation for all men, so one act of righteousness leads to justification and life for all men" (Romans 5:18).

The word "justified" means "found not guilty." As a child of the King, where do we begin when we feel guilty, even after we have confessed our sin?

On my search through Scripture, the following passage shed some light and confirmed that remaining in guilt is not what God has for his children. This passage is one of my favorites.

In the year that King Uzziah died I saw the Lord sitting upon a throne, high and lifted up; and the train of his robe filled the temple. Above him stood the seraphim. Each had six wings: with two he covered his face, and with two he covered his feet, and with two he flew. And one called to another and said:

"Holy, holy, holy is the Lord of hosts;
the whole earth is full of his glory!"

And the foundations of the thresholds shook at the voice of him who called, and the house was filled with smoke. And I said: "Woe is me! For I am lost; for I am a man of unclean lips, and I dwell in the midst of a people of unclean lips; for my eyes have seen the King, the Lord of hosts!"

Then one of the seraphim flew to me, having in his hand a burning coal that he had taken with tongs from the altar. And he touched my mouth and said: "Behold, this has touched your lips; your guilt is taken away, and your sin atoned for." (Isaiah 6:1–7)

Did you catch that? Our guilt is taken away! Hallelujah! (Join me in a happy dance.)

Isaiah was a righteous, godly man by all outward appearance. When he saw God in his splendor and holiness, every fiber of his being cried out, "Unworthy." Isaiah was keenly aware of his transgressions and lowly state before the Almighty. Isaiah's sin burned away because the fire of judgment consumed his sin. Once Isaiah had been convicted of his sin and cleansed from his guilt, he was ready to serve God. In fact, he volunteered. My heart longs to say the words Isaiah proclaimed in verse 8: "And I heard the voice of the Lord saying, 'Whom shall I send, and who will go for us?' Then I said, 'Here I am! Send me.'"

The forgiveness of God leads to thankful service. We still sin and sometimes can't shake the guilty feelings. What do we do? Let's learn from Paul.

The apostle Paul persecuted believers. He was on the road to Damascus to retrieve more Christians to lead to the slaughter by stoning. He had a life-altering encounter with Jesus. He, of all people, had a reason to struggle with guilt. He penned these words: "There is therefore now no condemnation for those who are in Christ Jesus" (Romans 8:1).

I wonder how often Paul claimed those words.

John, the disciple Jesus loved, stated: "If we confess our sins, he is faithful and just to forgive us our sins and to cleanse us from all unrighteousness" (1 John 1:9).

This is truth. We need to agree with God that our action or thought was sin and ask him to provide the strength to walk in righteousness. We must believe the truth and claim the promise for ourselves. We must not be swayed by fickle emotion, but instead, drive the final nail in guilt's coffin by grateful service to the Lord

The release from guilty feelings may not happen immediately. We must allow the Word to work its truth into our soul.

Once I allowed the Word to penetrate my heart and live by truth and not feeling, I began to focus on my Abba and not myself. I claimed his promises: "Let us draw near to God with a sincere heart and with the full assurance that faith brings, having our hearts sprinkled to cleanse us from a guilty conscience and having our bodies washed with pure water" (Hebrews 10:22 NIV).

Many emotions can overtake us and cause doubt, worry, and sin. A balanced view of our emotions is vital for victory over sin.

God gave us feelings as a barometer. We experience love, anger, joy, embarrassment, fear, anxiety, and so on. Our reaction to emotion must be controlled by the Holy Spirit as we compare each emotion with God's Word. The apostle Paul understood this: "We destroy arguments and every lofty opinion raised against the knowledge of God, and take every thought captive to obey Christ" (2 Corinthians 10:5).

It's not a sin to have negative emotions, but the negative feelings and emotions can lead to disobedience. James, the half-brother of Jesus, explains perfectly the path from temptation to actually sinning: "But each person is tempted when he is lured and enticed by his own desire. Then desire when it has conceived gives birth to sin, and sin when it is fully grown brings forth death" (James 1:14–15).

The reason temptation has its claws in us is because of our fallen nature. Satan tries to corrupt our desire to serve God by luring us with worldly pleasures. We give him too much credit for his power to tempt us. We fail to recognize that we are drawn away by our desires. Satan's great strategy in temptation is to convince us the pursuit of our corrupt desires will somehow produce life and goodness for us. Let's remember Satan comes to steal, kill, and destroy. Jesus gives us life eternal.

The thief comes only to steal and kill and destroy. I came that they may have life and have it abundantly. (John 10:10)

James gives us a promise: "Blessed is the man who endures temptation; for when he has been approved, he will receive the crown of life which the Lord has promised to those who love him" (James 1:12).

The truth is, our feelings may lead us astray, but standing firm on the truth reaps eternal rewards.

In the next chapter, we will do a mini theology lesson on the Word. Please persevere; don't let the word "theology" scare you. Theo-, which means god in Greek. The suffix -logy means "the study of," so theology literally means "the study of god." I want to know God more intimately, don't you? The best way to know him is to read Scripture.

The Word must transform our hearts and minds; it's vital for change. The truth is mandatory to release us from the chains of guilt, shame, and lies that lead to complaining. Scripture gives strength in our weakness. The Word works with the Holy Spirit to ignite a fire in us. The magnificent result? We shine. We will be a beacon of God's love and forgiveness. We must transform to help change the world.

Are you ready for a change? Let's go.

===========================

Memory verse
Isaiah 6:7, "And he touched my mouth and said: 'Behold, this has touched your lips; your guilt is taken away, and your sin atoned for.'"

Light reflection questions:

1. How did Isaiah react to the holiness of God? Why?

2. What does "justified" mean?

3. Should we trust our feelings? Why or why not?

Work the Word

I believed the lies my father told me.

"You are stupid. You don't even know how to make a bed."

I was four at the time, and my dad wanted me to make my bed with military precision. I still remember the brown and tan blanket with a checkerboard pattern. The lines on the top of the pillow had to connect with the lines of the blanket on the rest of the bed. My dad would squint his eyes, and if the contour of the lines was not even, he would tear the bed apart and make me do it again.

There were many times that my dad left us outside all day. If he remembered, he slipped a peanut butter sandwich through a slit in the screen door.

"You are animals. You need to stay outside. Now eat."

My father left when I was ten. His tormenting words remained an echo in my heart for the next twenty years.

I lived life with the belief I had no purpose. I convinced myself I was unlovable and had to make people like me. I became codependent on men. I found my identity and purpose in relationships. Men found me attractive, fun, and smart. Once they got to know me, they ran for the hills. No man wants a clingy whiner who suspects him of cheating. I engulfed them like a cloud of despair. They could not breathe without me knowing. My indulgence in self-loathing sabotaged each relationship. Even as a new believer, I still tried to find my identity in a man. My focus was marriage, and I knew my priorities were out of whack.

I began to memorize Scripture. The Word gradually worked out the attitude of self-hate and replaced it with a Christ-centered view. I am not the only believer who has experienced the life-changing effects of the Word.

Peter, an apostle of Christ, acted impulsively before learning pinpoint focus from Jesus. His emotions were finally controlled by the Holy Spirit instead of his flesh.

The apostle Paul changed his attitude about Christians when he met their leader on the road to Damascus. He learned to save souls instead of killing bodies.

These men knew the Word intimately, and the course of their lives changed with their attitude adjusted.

John 1 states that Jesus is the Word, and the Word became flesh and dwelt among us.

As a new believer, I said to myself, "If Jesus is the Word and I am to follow him and become like him, I must memorize the Word."

I desired to know the one who died for me. Knowing the Word means knowing him.

"Jesus is the same yesterday today and forever," the writer of Hebrews testifies, so the Word is reliable and true. However, some don't believe Scripture is inerrant and true. They don't take the word of God seriously. There are anorexic Christians walking the earth content with weak knees and feeble arms. They don't want to understand the importance of knowing Christ through the Word. That may seem harsh, but it's true. I know when I'm not in the Word, I feel spiritually sick. Think of the strongest Christians you know—I bet they memorize the Word.

We must feed on the Word to grow strong. Deuteronomy 8:3 says, "[M]an does not live by bread alone, but man lives by every word that comes from the mouth of the Lord." Jesus quoted this verse in Matthew 4:4 when Satan tempted him in the desert.

Jesus was famished and tired. He could have called all the angels to fight the battle. He did not. He used the mighty, living Word. If the Word is good enough for Jesus, it's good enough for us.

We have an enemy who does not want us to know our Savior. He does everything in his power to keep us weak and defeated. We must fight the battle with the Word as Jesus did. We'll learn more about Satan and his evil schemes in an upcoming chapter.

Jesus quoted the Old Testament more than thirty times, proving we must grasp Scripture and not let go. That is why I have so many Scripture references in this book.

Scripture is what set this captive free, and I desire freedom for all my brothers and sisters in Christ. Better still, God desires it for all his children.

Now the Lord is the Spirit, and where the Spirit of the Lord is, there is freedom. (2 Corinthians 3:17)

The Holy Spirit needs ammunition to fight against the flesh, the world, and the devil. The Word is that ammunition. It's the sword in our arsenal of weapons against sin. The Word gives us wisdom and power to live a life pleasing to God.

For the word of God is alive and active. Sharper than any double-edged sword, it penetrates even to dividing soul and spirit, joints, and marrow; it judges the thoughts and attitudes of the heart. (Hebrews 4:12 NIV)

Our goal is to shine like stars in this dark world, so we must consume the Word—make it a part of our being. We will not be joyful, strong, courageous, and free without the Word of God.

Now, let's establish that the Word of God is true and reliable. This may be a review for you; stick with me. This review will solidify the truth in our heart and mind.

The Bible claims to be the inspired Word of God: "All Scripture is breathed out by God and profitable for teaching, for reproof, for correction, and for training in righteousness" (2 Timothy 3:16).

God breathed his Word into the scribes, through the Holy Spirit, who, in turn, penned the Holy Scriptures. Each writer kept his personality while the Holy Spirit guided each person to write the truth.

[K]nowing this first of all, that no prophecy of Scripture comes from someone's own interpretation. For no prophecy was ever produced by the will of man, but men spoke from God as they were carried along by the Holy Spirit. (2 Peter 1:20–21)

Imagine being one of the prophets or scribes. I would tremble at the thought of a mistake. There were strict rules put in place so the transcription would be without error. The scribe had to use clean animal skin. Black ink was the only acceptable color, prepared from a special recipe. Scribes were required to take a ceremonial bath before the first stroke. It was mandatory to use a fresh quill each time they began to write the name of God. They would repeat the cleansing and take a new quill each time they wrote his name. I confess, I sometimes lack reverence for the Word and the name of God. My prayer is to learn from the scribes when it comes to acknowledging the holiness of our Abba. God made sure his Word was protected and transcribed correctly.

God wrote the Ten Commandments with his hand. "And he gave to Moses, when he had finished speaking with him on Mount Sinai, the two tablets of the testimony, tablets of stone, written with the finger of God" (Exodus 31:18).

God spoke to us through the prophets and now through his Son, who is the Word: "Long ago, at many times and in many ways, God spoke to our fathers by the prophets, but in these last days he has spoken to us by his Son, whom he appointed the heir of all things, through whom also he created the world" (Hebrews 1:1–2).

The apostle Paul wrote.

For I would have you know, brothers, that the gospel that was preached by me is not man's gospel. For I did not receive it from any man, nor was I taught it, but I received it through a revelation of Jesus Christ. (Galatians 1:11–12)

The Holy Spirit spoke the word.

Brothers, the Scripture had to be fulfilled, which the Holy Spirit spoke beforehand by the mouth of David concerning Judas. (Acts 1:16)

We see throughout Scripture that God the Father, God the Son, and God the Holy Spirit had a hand in with the Word.

There is much more written about this in the Bible. However, we want to establish that the Word is reliable and true. Only the Word can truly change our attitude.

I've experienced loving guidance from the Word—a nudge in the right direction and a strong spiritual knock when I was in blatant sin. God's Word is living. I have felt a hug through his promises, gained wisdom from Proverbs, and learned how to love my enemies from Scripture.

I began this book with the story of how my bad attitude needed an adjustment. That morning, as I studied, God showed me more. I prayed, *Lord, you are so awesome to show me that only the Word can change my attitude. I love acrostics, so can you give me one for the word "attitude?"*

I doubted he would. Remember, I woke up cranky and depressed. I thought the challenge was too great. Have you ever challenged the Lord? Be honest.

He proved me wrong. I got the Holy Ghost goosebumps when he revealed this acrostic for "attitude."

A: A
T: thought
T: that
I: ignites
T: true
U: undivided
D: devotion
E: every time.

God put me in my place. I had to repent of my unbelief. I marveled at his wisdom. What a mighty God we serve. He truly can do anything!

This brought to mind of one of my favorite verses from the Old Testament. I pray it for my son and others. "And you, my son Solomon, acknowledge the God of your father, and serve him with wholehearted devotion and with a willing mind, for the Lord searches every heart and understands every desire and every thought" (1 Chronicles 28:9 NIV).

David says this before he commissioned his son to build the temple. Some versions state that God understands the motives behind every thought. Now that's scary. At times I don't even understand my motives. I do know my motives have not always been pure. However, the Word can change motives and thoughts.

Scientists claim that our brains can grasp only one thought at a time. I have ADHD (attention deficit hyperactivity disorder), and it feels like my synapses are in overdrive. Thoughts run through my head like planes trying to land at a busy airport. It's my job to select which planes land. As a friend explained it, we are the control tower, and our thoughts are like airplanes.

We can choose to allow the biblical thoughts to land, and the lies, like enemy planes, to crash and burn. It seems drastic, but we must kill those thoughts before they have a chance to land and attack. One of the most stressful jobs in this world is an air traffic controller, especially during wartime, and you and I, my friend, are in a spiritual battle. It is a continual war of the mind. Like anyone who works in a control tower, we must be trained. Enemy planes want to test us and try to land. We must learn to spot them right away. We must wave them off or let them run out of fuel, wreck, and disintegrate. Allowing them to land could be catastrophic.

When I was in the Navy, I worked in top secret communications. The communications officer and I were tasked to set the IFF (Identification Friend or Foe) cryptology equipment. Each day had a new code to identify planes that crossed into the continental United States airspace. If an IFF interrogation receiver gets no reply or an invalid signal from an incoming IFF system, the aircraft must be challenged by government authorities. Are they friend or foe?

In the 1980s, the IFF equipment was bulky and tedious to set up. Precision and accuracy were of the utmost importance in setting the tiny pins in place. One morning, our C-130 crew flew from Hawaii to California. As we crossed into US airspace, we received communication to identify ourselves. We had all the proper communication codes but our IFF was wrong. How could this be? Our officer set the pins that morning. After a few attempts to convince air traffic control we were friendly, we looked out the aircraft window to see an F-14 fighter jet. It escorted us to the Naval base. If our plane did not have the proper markings or our secondary radio communication to prove us to be genuine, our plane would have been shot out of the air.

As Christians, we also have an IFF—the Holy Spirit working with the Bible. We must use this IFF to determine if our thoughts are friends or foes—truths or lies. The process of IFF is the process of renewing our mind. "Do not be conformed to this world, but be transformed by the renewal of your mind, that by testing you may discern what is the will of God, what is good and acceptable and perfect" (Romans 12:2).

We grow to know the will of our Savior more through this process. We can then also spot the enemy's lies and win the battle because we know the Word.

The enemy planes are familiar, and the pilot is Satan or his minions. We must get rid of them. We can no longer allow them to land. Our old self let the enemy planes land, fuel, and attack. The new self destroys the planes with the Word. Those planes crash and burn. In fact, Paul tells us how to get rid of them: "[A]ssuming that you have heard about him and were taught in him, as the truth is in Jesus, to put off your old self, which belongs to your former manner of life and is corrupt through deceitful desires, and to be renewed in the spirit of your minds, and to put on the new self, created after the likeness of God in true righteousness and holiness" (Ephesians 4:21–24).

The original word for "to be renewed" is *anneneo* ("to be spiritually transformed"). This word is only used once in the Bible. "To be spiritually transformed" means to take on a new mind and only allow purified friendly planes to land. These are aircraft filtered through IFF by the truth of the Word.

Put off old means once and for all. Paul is essentially saying, "Stop. Change your behavior, and do it now." He commands us to remove the garment of stink, filth, and sin, and to put on our true identity, which is Christ.

Imagine if your shirt caught fire—you would rip it off your body. That is the imagery Paul declares here concerning our old sin nature. Rip it off!

"To put on" is a verb meaning "to be made new in attitude." In the original Greek, it means an ongoing action where God will help you. This process is called "sanctification." Jesus acknowledges the importance of this process of change when he prays for our sanctification: "Sanctify them in the truth; your word is truth" (John 17:17).

Let's take a moment and thank him for praying for us. Jesus beseeches the Father on our behalf. The cross was on his mind; he struggled with the thought of Calvary, but he prayed for us in the midst of his angst. What a glorious Savior.

Sanctification is the process of being made like Christ through the Holy Spirit's work in us. We need the Holy Spirit to understand the Word of God. "When the Spirit of truth comes, he will guide you into all the truth, for he will not speak on his own authority, but whatever he hears he will speak, and he will declare to you the things that are to come" (John 16:13).

Applying the Word of God without the power of the Spirit is like using a chainsaw without pulling the chord. Hopeless.

The Spirit brings freedom to understand the Word. Who wants freedom? I do! Freedom from the penalty of the law, freedom from whining, guilt, and shame. To get this freedom, we must know the word of God.

The apostle Paul writes about his struggle:

> For I know that nothing good dwells in me, that is, in my flesh. For I have the desire to do what is right, but not the ability to carry it out. For I do not do the good I want, but the evil I do not want is what I keep on doing. Now if I do what I do not want, it is no longer I who do it, but sin that dwells within me.

> So I find it to be a law that when I want to do right, evil lies close at hand. For I delight in the law of God, in my inner being, but I see in my members another law waging war against the law of my mind and making me captive to the law of sin that dwells in my members. Wretched man that I am! Who will deliver me from this body of death? Thanks be to God through Jesus Christ our Lord! So then, I myself serve the law of God with my mind, but with my flesh I serve the law of sin. (Romans 7:18–25)

Paul admits the war raged in him. We must admit it also.

A story is told of a dog handler in Alaska, who owned two dogs—one black and the other white. Once a month, he brought the dogs to town and fought them against one another. The people of the town would bet on which dog they think would win. Each time the dogs fought, a different dog would win. The fights were not fixed, in fact, they were quite ferocious, but the owner always bet on the winning dog. When he finally stopped fighting the dogs, the people asked him, "How is it that you always know which dog is going to win?"

"That's easy," he replied, "the one I feed the most."

We must choose to feed our spirit and not our flesh.

It is a scientific fact that the brain can only contemplate one thought at a time. How glorious would it be if our brain would automatically think a thought that ignites true undivided devotion every time toward our God? We must feed the Spirit for that to occur. We must let the Word devour our sinful nature.

Let's commit to memorizing his Word not because it's expected of us but because we desire to be more like Christ. God wants us to have peace, love, joy, and wisdom in abundance. If we struggle with a sinful lifestyle, we must fight it with the Word.

I struggle with pride. I got a concordance, looked up every verse on pride, and memorized them. This helps me put off the old nature and put on the new! I'm still convicted at times, especially when people compliment my speaking or teaching. The Spirit reminds me of the Bible verses, and I don't allow those enemy planes of self-praise to land. I wave them off by giving God the glory for empowering me to serve him.

The enemy planes of self-loathing still attacked, however. Those were harder to recognize.

My old self was convinced I was useless, unlovable, and ugly. When meeting me, I seemed confident and happy. I had a false facade of joy. Deep inside, I felt desolate. God revealed my wrong thinking. I memorized these two verses and quoted them to myself daily:

[E]ven as he chose us in him before the foundation of the world, that we should be holy and blameless before him. (Ephesians 1:4)

Your eyes saw my unformed substance, in your book were written, every one of them the days that were formed for me, when as yet there was none of them. (Psalm 139:16)

The sanctification process blossomed into truth as I realized God chose me for his reasons alone. It was not anything that I could mess up. Thank you, Lord!

I added more memory verses:

But to all who did receive him, who believed in his name, he gave the right to become children of God, who were born, not of blood nor of the will of the flesh nor of the will of man, but of God. (John 1:12–13)

Wow, God wants me here. My biological father did not choose me, but the God of the universe chose me. I am his, and he is mine. My identity is in my Abba, not an abusive sinner.

My attitude change was gradual. There were days when I would quote these verses with no emotion; the Spirit was still at work. Slowly, I began to see myself as God sees me.

Now I know my purpose is to glorify my Abba Father in heaven. At times, I still struggle with feelings of inadequacy, and I murmur, but I claim his promises.

The light of the Word shed truth into my wrong way of thinking and changed it into God's way of thinking. He will do it for anyone who seeks his face.

The Word combats enemy planes. Scripture is a light unto our path and brings refinement so we can shine bright in this dark world.

Let's commit to learning the verses in this book. The next chapter gives us tips to memorize Scripture and to make it a part of our being. Join me and obtain the tools to stop complaining and shine.

============================

Memory verse
Ephesians 4:22–23, "[T]o put off your old self, which belongs to your former manner of life and is corrupt through deceitful desires, and to be renewed in the spirit of your minds."

Light reflection questions:

1. What was the practice of biblical scribes when they transcribed the name of God?

2. Why is it important to memorize the Word of God?

3. What do we need to take off to be made new in the attitude of our mind?

Memorize the Word

Hi, my name is Forgetful. Birthdays, names, and special dates elude me. Can you relate? Information swims in a dark hole I call my memory. I struggle to find the information at the moment I need it, only to have the information reveal itself at another time. How can I memorize Scripture with a brain that won't work?

In my travels, I am blessed to speak to numerous women. Scripture memorization is one of the most difficult and painful disciplines they encounter. I understand the dilemma. Many give up and resign to saying:

"I am too old."

"My brain doesn't work."

"I don't have the time."

"It's not that important."

The Bible commands us to hide the Word in our heart and be transformed by the renewing of the mind. Can we commit Scripture to memory when our mind is unresponsive to any prompting?

We can memorize words, to songs, phone numbers, social security numbers, our address, and more, so why not Scripture?

Brain fog hinders my memory. I have fibromyalgia and chronic fatigue. Names are hard to remember, so I didn't think I could memorize the Word of God. I asked God to help me. The first portion of Scripture I memorized was Isaiah 6:1–8. Then I memorized Revelation 4. How could a foggy brain commit nineteen verses to memory in less than two months? Work and repetition.

I read each verse ten times, then wrote it on a sticky note. I added a verse each day. Each day, I read the entire note ten times. I switched to a notepad and rewrote the entire segment of Scripture. It took diligence. I also memorized a verse to empower me to endure: "I can do all things through him who strengthens me" (Philippians 4:13).

At the same time I asked God to help me memorize his Word, I was blessed with a mentor, Sue. We attended the same church. She required me to memorize a verse per week as we studied the Bible.

"How can I do that? My brain doesn't work well."

"You can do it because the Holy Spirit will help you," Sue replied.

To make Bible memorization fun, we decided to memorize verses that corresponded with my birthday, August 2 (08/02). My first verses were Deuteronomy 8:2–3. I was blessed to memorize a verse quoted by Jesus. He recites Deuteronomy 8:3: "[T]hat he might make you know that man does not live by bread alone, but man lives by every word that comes from the mouth of the Lord."

I knew the importance of the Word from my first memory verse. Sue encouraged me. "It is the will of God that we know

Jesus. The only way to know him intimately is to consume the Word and make it a daily part of life," she said.

We memorized many verses together. My mind absorbed the Word like a dry sponge soaks water. God did help me remember his Word. He will help you too. I want to share some practical ways to accomplish this. I wrote the verse on a sticky note and put it on the dashboard of my car. When I was at a stoplight, I would read it. There are various other ways to memorize Scripture as well. I'm not asking you to learn one verse per week. Just think, if you committed to memory one verse per month, you would have twelve swords in your weapons arsenal to fight the spiritual battle we face daily. Remember, the Word is called the sword of the Spirit. Before you start memorizing, ask God for help.

Teach me, O LORD, the way of your statutes; and I will keep it to the end. (Psalm 119:33)

Direct me in the path of your commands, for there I find delight. (Psalm 119:35)

Memorizing God's Word brings obedience and healing and helps the believer shine, not whine.

Let's look at three methods to memorize: music, index cards or sticky notes, and household decorations.

Music is a great way to learn Scripture. We have a series of audiotapes with Scripture songs. I have committed ten verses to memory from listening to them. My son loves them, and we listen to them in the car. My favorite is, "Evening and morning and at noon will I pray and cry aloud He will hear my voice." God has used this verse, Psalm 55:17 KJV, to minister to me and others. A huge bonus, Satan hates the Word and praise music. Listening to Scripture songs will make him flee.

Index cards or sticky notes are easy to carry. You can put them on a desk at work, stick it to the bathroom mirror as you get ready for the day, pull them out of your purse while waiting in line, put it on the treadmill when you work out, or stick it to your dashboard in the car. I have done each of these. One day I pulled my card out in line at the supermarket. The guy behind me glanced over my shoulder. I heard an, "Ah-ha!" from behind me. I did not turn around because I was next in line. I don't know what effect it had on him, but I do know the Word does not come back void.

Scripture art and plaques are placed in strategic places in my house. The shelf over the kitchen sink has a small painted rock with the Scripture, "I am the vine; you are the branches. Whoever abides in me and I in him . . . bears much fruit" (John 15:5). I remember the rest of that verse although it's not painted on the rock, "[F]or apart from me you can do nothing." Grapes are painted on it to add color and decoration. This verse reminds me that I need God and his Spirit to accomplish my daily routine.

I almost purchased a beautiful piece of art. I had just moved into a new home. I shopped for a decorative piece to match my bird shower curtain. A beautiful plaque had "follow your heart" painted on it. I thought I found the perfect adornment for the bathroom. It had the same blue hue and a bird. Score! As I went to purchase my treasure, I hesitated. A Bible verse came to mind: "The heart is deceitful above all things, and desperately sick; who can understand it?" (Jeremiah 17:9).

I knew I had to leave the art behind. I went home empty-handed and studied the Bible. Sometimes memorizing verses will drive you deeper into the Word.

God wants us to follow him as he changes our heart.

I did find a cross to complement my shower curtain; it looks perfect.

There are other places to keep Scripture. Use a verse for your wallpaper on your phone, tablet, or laptop. There are t-shirts, hats, and jewelry with scripture. Be creative.

Memorizing God's Word helps us to be obedient: "I have stored up your word in my heart, that I might not sin against you" (Psalm 119:11).

How will we know what God expects from us if we don't know his Word? There have been times I wish I didn't know Scripture, or at least certain verses, especially when I was angry at someone who wronged me. I wanted that person to feel the pain I felt. The Holy Spirit reminded me, "[I]n your anger do not sin." (Ephesians 4:26) I was so upset because I knew the Lord was right. However, I said, "Then you yell at him, God! Maybe he'll listen to you."

Have you bitten your tongue and made it bleed to save a relationship? The next day I was glad I listened to the Spirit and did not verbally lash out.

* * *

I spent three months in Honduras assisting a missionary in her medical clinic. I memorized some verses in Spanish. Many of the verses I studied came to mind as I removed stitches from a young boy's face, helped a mother bring her child into the world, dispensed medicine, saved a drunk man from the impact of an oncoming car when he fell into the road, endured the theft of my new watch, and looked to the night sky as stars twinkled. God's Word sustained me through some difficult days serving him in a third world country.

I was met with heartbreak when I returned home from Honduras. The Spirit whispered verses of comfort and healing as I tried to recover. The relationship with a man I thought I would marry was over, and my body was rendered useless from fibromyalgia and chronic fatigue. I had no job. I wondered what God wanted me to do. Energy and strength escaped my body. I had enough for one task per day, either dishes or dusting. I laid on the couch desperate to hear from God but had no desire to go to church or read the Bible. Even my best friend told me I was in sin because I missed church for two weeks in a row. I begged God to heal and hug me. I felt a warm sensation, like an embrace, and the Spirit reminded me of a verse that I memorized years prior to this enchanted encounter with God: "The Lord will guide you always; he will satisfy your needs in a sun-scorched land and will strengthen your frame. You will be like a well-watered garden; like a spring whose waters never fail" (Isaiah 58:11 NIV)

I knew my heavenly Father was there for me, and I just needed to rest and wait for restoration.

The Spirit will bring to our minds verses to help us in a time of need, but it has to be in our brain first.

The prophet Jeremiah stood in the ruins of his people. He previously warned them to turn back to God; they did not listen. As he gazed upon the bodies of dead women and children after enemies raided their city and laughed at the destruction, he laments: "I remember my affliction and my wandering, the bitterness, and the gall. I well remember them, and my soul is downcast within me. Yet this I call to mind and therefore I have hope: Because of the Lord's great love we are not consumed, for his compassions never fail, they are new every morning; great is your faithfulness. I say to myself, 'The Lord is my portion; therefore, I will wait for him.'" (Lamentations 3:19–24).

He remembers the goodness of the Lord in the midst of tragedy. As a prophet, he knew God's Word. Memorization is so important. The Word will renew our mind from bad memories or put them in perspective with God's truth, loving-kindness, and justice.

When the enemy whispers to me and tries to remind me of my past, I recite the Word out loud, "I am fearfully and wonderfully made, and no weapon formed against me shall prosper" (Psalm 139:14; Isaiah 54:17)

The apostle Peter beseeches believers to remember the Word, "Dear friends, this is now my second letter to you. I have written both of them as reminders to stimulate you to wholesome thinking. I want you to recall the words spoken in the past by the holy prophets and the command given by our Lord and Savior through your apostles" (2 Peter 3:1–2 NIV).

The apostle Peter believed in the transforming effect of the Word. Scripture memorization is important for obedience to God. We can say we love God, but if we do not know his Word, how can we obey him?

For this is the love of God, that we keep his commandments. And his commandments are not burdensome. (1 John 5:3).

The desire to obey and love God grows cold and stagnant when we do not remain in his Word. When we love someone, we look for ways to serve or please that person, even during difficult times. Jesus reminds the people of God's Great Commandment and expounded on it: "You shall love the Lord your God with all your heart and with all your soul and with all your mind. This is the great and first commandment. And a second is like it: You shall love your neighbor as yourself. On these two commandments depend all the Law and the Prophets" (Matthew 22:37–40).

I loved others more than myself. I served and gave of my time and money to help those in need, yet I did it hesitantly. I prayed and asked God, *What about me? When do I get to be served, loved, and cared for?*

As I memorized Scriptures on God's love for me, I began to see myself through his eyes and appreciate the masterpiece he created in me.

For we are God's masterpiece. He has created us anew in Christ Jesus, so we can do the good things he planned for us long ago. (Ephesians 2:10 NLT).

My selfish attitude vanishes in the light of the knowledge of Scripture.

Scripture memorization is vital for living a life of godliness and power. The Word penetrates our heart and works out the sin and pain. Job knew this when his friends tried to help him.

He uncovers the deeps out of darkness and brings deep darkness to light. (Job 12:22)

Previously, Zophar disparaged Job for not knowing God and likened Job to an empty-headed man. In the days of Job, men loved intellectual discussions. This made them feel important. Job offered that he did indeed know God and that the Lord is great in wisdom and strength.

Job knew that God has power to reveal the darkness that resides in a man's heart and the ability to take away the understanding of even great men. When he does this, the men grope in the dark without light. Job revealed that the wisdom and understanding of man are dependent upon God.

Even King David, a sinner, yet a man after God's heart, knew that without memorizing the Word, he would lack the counsel he needed to rule the kingdom and live a life worthy of his calling. He penned over 180 verses about the Word of God. Psalm 119 alone has 176 verses.

Here are just a few verses from the heart of King David. May we have a heart that desires to commit the Word to memory.

How can a young man keep his way pure?
By guarding it according to your word.
With my whole heart I seek you;
let me not wander from your commandments!
I have stored up your word in my heart,
that I might not sin against you.
Blessed are you, O Lord;
teach me your statutes!
With my lips I declare
all the rules of your mouth.
In the way of your testimonies I delight
as much as in all riches.
I will meditate on your precepts
and fix my eyes on your ways.

I will delight in your statutes;
I will not forget your word. (Psalm 119:9–16)

Yes, King David made many mistakes, just like we will. However, his motive was to please God. The more David knew the Word, the more he desired to serve his Master.

Will you join me in memorizing Scripture?

If the thought of it intimidates you, start slowly. Pick one verse or paragraph and set a reasonable time frame to keep yourself on track. Scripture memorization is an investment of time and energy, but the return is far more valuable and reaps eternal rewards. God will help you train your brain. The light of the Word illuminates you to shine.

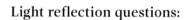

Memory verse
Psalm 119:11, "I have stored up your word in my heart, that I might not sin against you."

Light reflection questions:

1. Why is Scripture memorization important?

2. Name two ways to commit the Bible to memory.

3. What is the Holy Spirit's role in Scripture memorization?

A: Always Pray

"But we will devote ourselves to prayer and to
the ministry of the word" (Acts 6:4).

The Journalistic Approach

"**Y**ou don't pray to Jesus; you pray to God in Jesus's name," an unfamiliar woman said to me as she released my hand and shook her head in disgust.

I attended a mission conference at a church in Connecticut with some members of my Rhode Island church. We broke into prayer groups and ended our individual group prayer. My prayer was, "Lord Jesus, please help those who are undergoing persecution. Thank you, Lord God, for hearing our prayers. In Jesus's name, amen."

"God hears all prayer, doesn't he?" I asked the group. I did not get an answer. The group disappeared to the next scheduled event, leaving me with questions and concerns. I was a new believer, eager to please God and talk to him. To pray in public did not scare me. I was talking to my Father in heaven. I had an audience of one. But this woman's words made me rethink the entire prayer process. Fear crept in.

Does God hear me? Is there a special key to prayer that unlocks the throne room of God? It was bad enough that I wrestled with thoughts of insignificance and unworthiness. Could it be I didn't know how to communicate with the only one who could help me? I had failed at earning my earthly father's love. Because I didn't speak God's language, could he even hear me? The rest of the day I faked a smile. The unknown woman's words of rejection and condemnation echoed in my head, fueling my despair.

As I matured in my walk, I learned that we pray to God in the name of Christ by the power of the Holy Spirit. God is a triune God. When we talk to one member, they all hear.

As a child struggles to learn how to form words into sentences, I too learned how to pray to my Abba. I know he hears me, like a parent; he clings to each word. Parents long to understand what their child is communicating. Our Abba bends his ear toward us like a parent who squats to embrace a child, pulls the child close, not wanting to miss a single word.

And this is the confidence that we have toward him, that if we ask anything according to his will he hears us. (1 John 5:14).

Because he inclined his ear to me, therefore I will call on him as long as I live. (Psalm 116:2)

God hears prayer. He heard my prayer in Connecticut, and he hears me now. He hears all of his children. What great comfort.

I didn't encounter the unknown woman again. I pray for her and others like her as we learn to communicate with our Father. May we be free to pray to God and not think we need a specific formula. He is our Daddy. We can approach him at any time with any need. God knows our heart. He even knows what we need before we ask.

And when you pray, do not heap up empty phrases as the Gentiles do, for they think that they will be heard for their many words. Do not be like them, for your Father knows what you need before you ask him. (Matthew 6:7–8)

As a speaker/teacher, I know that defining the terms is important. A phrase or word may mean something different to you than it does to me. Before we get into the meat of the specific prayers, let's define prayer.

What is prayer?

D. L. Moody, an evangelist and founder of Moody Bible Institute, asked kids in Scotland, "What is prayer?" Five hundred little hands went up.

Moody pointed to one child who said, "Prayer is the offering up of our desires unto God with the confession of our standard with a baneful acknowledgment of his mercies."

I wish I knew that as a child. I didn't know the definition of "baneful," let alone the meaning of prayer.

The Bible is filled with statements on prayer. Let's review a few verses before we dive into the next portion.

The prayer of a righteous person has great power as it is working. (James 5:16)

[P]ray without ceasing. (1 Thessalonians 5:17)

Finally, brothers, pray for us, that the word of the Lord may speed ahead and be honored. (2 Thessalonians 3:1)

Humans have been able to communicate with God from the beginning of time. Adam and Eve walked with God and spoke directly to him. After the fall, communication was no longer face to face.

At that time, people began to call upon the name of the Lord. (Genesis 4:26)

Prayer means to ask for something. So how do we go about conversing with the king of the universe? Let's put on the hat of a journalist for answers.

When a good news reporter investigates a story, that person retrieves and analyzes the facts by answering the following questions: who, what, where, when, why, and how? We will briefly answer each of these questions about prayer. I encourage you to do an in-depth study on your own or with a group.

Who Prays?
Everyone has said a prayer once or twice in their lives. There is a saying, "There are no atheists in foxholes." We tend to call out

to God when we are in trouble. However, anyone can call on the name of the Lord, even children.

"Do you ask God for help while you're at school?" I asked my son as we walked home from the bus stop.

"No, Mom. I get so busy that I forget to pray."

My heart sank. My son and I read the Bible and listened to Christian music each morning at breakfast. I taught him how to pray. I felt like a failure.

As I silently prayed, God reminded me that parents are to teach and guide, which takes time and patience. Kids don't always get the lesson the first time, and neither do adults.

I made my son an afternoon snack.

"Do you know that you can talk to God all day?"

"Yes, I will try to remember. I didn't think God listened to kids," my son said as he placed his backpack on the floor.

As he munched on the grapes I said, "Remember, Jesus told the disciples, 'Let the little children come to me.'"

"YES! I can't wait to meet him in heaven."

"So, let's pray every morning before you go to school."

The next morning my husband and I held my son's hands and prayed with him.

I took his beautiful face, looked into his eyes, and said, "Call on the name of the Lord; he will help you and listen to whatever you want to tell him."

I gave him a kiss on the cheek.

My son walked out the door singing, "I will call upon the Lord who is worthy to be praised."

My heart filled with joy as I hummed the tune all day.

A kiss and a prayer are our morning ritual now. It helps us to remember that we can call on the name of the Lord all day.

Our home is more joyful as we practice praying all day. The busyness of life still creeps in, trying to rob me of my constant contact with my Abba. He is so good to remind me to call on his name. He is waiting for you and me to spend time with him.

The Lord is near to all who call on him, to all who call on him in truth. (Psalm 145:18)

What Do We Pray?

Anything. Prayer is making our requests known to God. We can talk to him about the weather, food, family, and concerns. Our prayers can include the Scriptures and his promises to us, because we serve a personal God.

Standing in the middle of Africa on a dry, dirt road at one o'clock in the morning was not my definition of fun. I had a sinus headache from all the agricultural burning in Togo. To add to the angst, my judgmental heart was taking over; no one was witnessing to the group of locals who gathered to watch our mission team try to fix a tire. White men don't usually drive through their village, let alone break down in the middle of the night, so every man and boy within a mile radius joined the growing crowd.

Five months prior, my mind was not on the trip to Africa. My baby was due March 6, 2001—a joyous surprise that kept me from going on the trip. We were very excited. I heard the heartbeat at thirteen weeks. With one baby already in heaven, I knew that God would not take this one too. After the sonogram, I met a friend for a movie at the IMAX theater. I felt dizzy and sick to my stomach. I attributed the symptoms to the 3-D movie and vertigo.

Two days later I was on the floor with stomach cramps. Another child gone, and my heart was in pieces. We now have two babies in heaven. We named our first Michael Corban ("a gift dedicated to God") and the second Talitha Grace ("little girl of grace"). Naming the babies gave us closure, even if we did not know the gender.

The medication I took for my headache began to work. I dragged myself out of the van onto the dirt road. As my eyes adjusted to the dark, I looked to my left, grass huts. We broke down in the middle of a village. In front of me I saw a few of my fellow missionaries trying to change the tire of the lead van. There were also some local tribesmen examining the situation. I loved how the locals wore Western attire—very clean and crisp. I wondered how they kept everything so nice amidst all the dirt. To my right, another group of men just watching.

I grabbed my husband's hand and said, "Let's go. God gave us these men to witness to." We walked up to the complete strangers and introduced ourselves. They were very happy to meet us. A few of the men understood English. I forgot about my sinus infection as we shared the good news of Jesus Christ. I sensed that they understood, but I wanted to make sure. We asked Pastor Mike, the local pastor traveling with us, to explain the gospel in their native language (Ewe and French).

As he explained the free gift of eternal life, a few men stepped back. I found out later that Pastor Mike asked them to walk away if they did not want to make a decision for Christ. He said, "This is a very important decision; do not do it if you are not committed."

Five men stayed and accepted Christ as Savior. Hallelujah! As we prayed, the Lord reminded me of the Sunday morning before we left for Africa.

I stood in the front of the church devastated, missing my unborn child. I prayed as tears wet the floor in front of me, *Lord, if I never have my own child, please give me babes in Christ when I go to Africa. I only want to serve you, Lord.*

As I stood there 4,900 miles away from home, the Lord spoke to my heart and said, *These are your babes in Christ.*

The men dispersed, our tire was fixed, and we finished our medical mission.

One year later we welcomed Michael Joseph Bisbano Jr. into the world, and Pastor Mike informed us that the men we witnessed to, my babes in Christ, served in their local church.

Where Do We Pray?

Anywhere. Jonah prayed from the belly of a large fish (Jonah 2.) David prayed in a cave (Psalm 142). Nehemiah prayed while standing before King Artaxerxes (Nehemiah 2:1–5).

I prayed as I hung from a seatbelt wondering, *What just happened?* My friend Dan was scheduled to drive back from our ski trip, but I drove because Dan injured his knee. Snow fell lightly on the mountain road causing slippery conditions. As I swerved to miss an oncoming car in my lane, the tires lost traction. My tire hit the edge of the road, and our Jeep flipped one and a half times landing on the passenger side doors. We watched cars drive by and stare at us as we hung sideways from our seatbelts. I released my belt and landed on the passenger door, now secured by the ground. I called out to God to bring someone to help. A tow truck arrived immediately. The driver of the truck just happened to live at the top of the mountain. We were not hurt in the accident. The Jeep landed on the only patch of ground on the entire mountainside. The rest of the roadside was a sheer cliff. I know God heard my prayer that day.

When Do We Pray?

Anytime. Psalm 55:17 states, "[E]vening and morning and at noon I utter my complaint and moan, and he hears my voice."

After the Jeep accident on the mountain, we were taken to the police station to wait for our ride home. A man began a conversation with me.

"I hear you kids are lucky to be alive. Your Jeep found the only grassy knoll on this here mountain."

"Yes, but I don't consider it luck."

"Ya don't? You're standing here aren't you?"

I was tired and still shaking a little as the Spirit prompted me to speak.

"Yes, let me explain. I don't believe in luck. God protected us. I thank him."

"You sound like my sister. She's been trying to get me to go to Bible study."

"Why don't you go?"

"Ahhh, that's nonsense."

"If it's nonsense, I would not be here talking to you. I believe God is calling you, my friend."

"It's too late for an ol' man like me."

I prayed, *Lord, help me to be loving yet bold,* as I looked at the wrinkles close around his furrowed brow.

"It's never too late; why don't you go to the next study? When is it?"

"Tonight. My sister would keel over if I walked in."

"Well, when she gets off the ground, she will give you a big hug."

"Ha! That's a good one. Still able to joke after that scary ride."

"Yes, I am blessed that we did not get hurt, or hurt anyone else."

"Nice talkin' to you, Miss. I wish you luck. Um, I mean God bless you."

"Same to you, sir."

I still pray for that man. I am convinced God used this difficult situation for his glory. We can pray whenever we need him.

Why Do We Pray?

To make our requests known to God, to praise him, and to communicate with him. He cares for us.

I learned this the hard way when my mouth would not stop bleeding. I had a skin graft taken from the roof of my mouth and placed at the base of a tooth to prevent the loss of that tooth. The initial surgery was not painful, just uncomfortable. The surgeon told me that it should heal quickly.

At the time of surgery, I was a new believer. I was learning how to pray. I did not pray for my mouth to heal. I thought it was too small and insignificant to God. He had bigger problems to solve, like world hunger.

It was time for my checkup. My report of increased pain, discomfort, and bleeding worried the surgeon.

"I don't know why you are not healing. Are you doing everything I asked you to do?"

"Yes," I said.

A still, small voice inside my head said, *Pray and ask me to heal you.*

I left the dental office with an appointment to return in five days.

I heard the voice again. *Pray and ask me to heal you.*

It couldn't be God. He had bigger concerns.

I headed to church for the prayer meeting. I never missed it. I loved to intercede on behalf of others and still do. As I sat in pain, blood at the corner of my mouth, I hesitated to ask for prayer, but the words echoed in my head, *Pray and ask me to heal you.*

After we prayed for our country, missionaries, and lost souls, I spoke. "My mouth has not healed from surgery. It's been over two weeks, and the surgeon is concerned. It's such a small thing. I don't even want to ask for prayer, but it's getting worse."

I fixed my eyes on the floor in front of me.

"Cherrilynn," my pastor said, "your heavenly Father is concerned about your mouth. He wants you to come to him with everything. Now go ahead and pray for yourself."

As I prayed for healing, the discomfort went away, and the bleeding subsided.

I returned to the surgeon.

"Your mouth looks so much better. What did you do?"

"I finally prayed."

How Do We Pray?
In the power of the Holy Spirit.

"Will you pray for me?" my friend asked. "My heart is broken, and I am lonely."

Deb shared her desire to be married as we walked the bike path.

"Let's pray now, Deb."

As I prayed, the Spirit filled my mouth with words I hesitated to say.

"You will be married within a year."

How could I utter those words? I don't want to be the catalyst that breaks my friend's heart.

Oh me of little faith.

We closed in prayer.

"Deb, the Spirit told me to pray that. I was hesitant."

"I'm not even dating anyone; Cherrilynn, how can that happen?"

"We'll leave it in God's hands for now."

Less than one year later, Deb married.

When we pray in the power of the Spirit, allowing him to speak in and through us, mighty things happen.

I know these are brief statements, but prayer is not meant to be complicated. God wants us to come to him without reservation. He hears our prayers. At times, he does not answer the way we think, and we may not understand until we get to heaven.

God answers prayers with yes, no, or wait. Every answer is filtered through his love. Prayer is a continual conscious contact with our maker. Praying his Word helps us to understand his desire for us. Knowing that our Lord loves us unconditionally and hears our prayers will enable us to cry out to him with our concerns, not whine to others. Now, let's learn how the Word eradicates the darkness and fills it with light.

=============================

Memory verse
Psalm 116:2, "Because he inclined his ear to me, therefore I will call on him as long as I live."

Light reflection questions:

1. Who can pray? Explain.

2. Why do we pray? Explain.

3. Where do we pray? Explain.

Surgical Prayer

To pray the Scriptures is to perform spiritual surgery in a person's innermost being. I experienced the sword of God's Word firsthand when I stormed the gates of heaven proclaiming the life-changing truths. My deepest desire—to know the love of God and makes it known to others. I aspired to have delicate discernment when I ministered.

My attitude, however, hindered me from fully being used by God. I needed to forgive my childhood abuser and see him as God sees him. I clung to my right to fight. I was wronged. I should be able to hold on to a grudge, right?

Wrong. I studied the prayers of Paul. Oh, to obtain the inner peace Paul had. He was flogged, shipwrecked, thrown into jail, and left for dead. He learned contentment and found peace amidst the trials. I wanted that peace. I prayed the Scripture for a changed heart. After all, the Scripture states it will change attitudes—and mine were obstinate.

The Spirit taught me to combine some of the apostle Paul's prayers into one prayer. The interweaving of the Scriptures produces powerful, poignant prayer. I began praying this prayer for myself and others. The working of the Word in me was like surgery. The sword of the Word lanced my tumors of sin and replaced them with a salve that heals. The truth transformed my hatred into love and my pain into possibilities.

The Scripture references are Ephesians 3:17–20; 1 Corinthians 13:4–8; and Philippians 1:9–11. I paraphrase the Scriptures for The Surgical Prayer.

Lord, I pray that out of your glorious riches you would strengthen us with power through your Spirit in our inner being so Christ may dwell in our hearts through faith, that we would be rooted and established in love—your love that is patient, kind, not envious, boastful, rude, or proud; your love that keeps no records of wrong and never fails. May we have the strength to comprehend the breadth, length, height, and depth of your love for us, and to know the love of Christ, which surpasses knowledge. I pray this so that our love may abound more and more with wisdom and depth of insight so that we can discern what is best and be found blameless on the day of Christ, Now to you—who is able to do above and beyond all we ask or imagine, according to the power at work within us—be glory in the church and in Christ Jesus throughout all generations forever and ever. Amen.

This prayer seems like a mouthful, but when earnestly prayed and believed, it will cause a radical change.

Let's dissect some of the words in the prayer to get the full impact of its power. The italicized word is the original Greek or Hebrew word.

"[T]hat we would be rooted and established in love."
Rooted: *rhizoo*: to cause to strike root; to strengthen with roots; to render firm; to fix; establish.
Established: *themelioo*: to lay the foundation; to found; to make stable; establish.

I think of a big oak tree, its roots secured deep into the soil. There is no moving it. When we are rooted and established in God's love, we know during the darkest, most tragic night, when the winds are whipping, God is there. His love grounds us. The prophet Jeremiah describes one who trusts in the Lord: "He is like a tree planted by streams of water that yields its fruit in its season, and its leaf does not wither. In all that he does, he prospers" (Psalm 1:3).

I desire the love of God to destroy all fear, doubt, and worry. I feared failure and doubted that God loved me. I learned that the deep love of Jesus will eradicate all fear: "There is no fear in love, but perfect love casts out fear" (1 John 4:18).

There are four different words used for love in the Greek language.

Storgē: a natural affection.
Phileō: friendship.
Eros: erotic or passionate love.
Agapē: sacrificial, unconditional love.

The love that Paul talks about here is *agapē*. Jesus proves his love for us through his sacrifice on the cross. When we pray that we would know this love and have it for others, we acknowledge what Christ accomplished at the cross, and in turn, we humble ourselves so that we may love in the power of the Spirit without hesitation or boundaries. This is a process.

Imagine knowing the full extent of God's love so that it becomes part of us. His love takes over our speech, thoughts, and actions. We don't have to wish for it; we have it in us, we must exercise this love and make it stronger.

As a wounded new believer, I still felt unlovable. I thought God had to love me because I was his child. I had a warped view of my Creator because of my abusive childhood. As I relentlessly prayed and sought the face of my Abba in heaven, he made me keenly aware of his love by giving me an overwhelming sense of joy, peace, and acceptance. I know it's because I prayed, memorized the Word, and asked him to reveal this to me. All these treasures are for you too. Don't stop praying. God hears you and will reward you.

I praise him and thank him for reminding me that he has poured his love into my heart through the Holy Spirit.

[A]nd hope does not put us to shame, because God's love has been poured into our hearts through the Holy Spirit who has been given to us. (Romans 5:5)

I don't have any excuse to hate. I can draw on the love that dwells in me. My attitude changed, especially my attitude toward my biological father.

Wanting my father to get what he deserved slowly disappeared as I saw his need for Christ. Holding hatred in my heart toward my abuser turned into a desire to forgive.

Over time, I felt no animosity toward the one who left the emotional scars. I even prayed for him. I no longer waited for the day I could laugh when something bad happened to him. I had compassion for him.

I was free from hatred toward my earthy father, because I prayed the surgical prayer for him and me. Freedom meant that I had to let go of my right to fight, and allow God to heal me and release the consequences of my dad's sin against me, to my heavenly Father.

We have no excuse for hatred, vengeance, or complacency. We have the power to love others as a child of the King.

Love is not only an emotion, but it is also a decision to obey God. Let's look at a few more words in our surgical prayer.

Patient: *makrothymeō*: be of a long spirit; not to lose heart; longsuffering.

Kind: *chrēsteuomai*: show oneself useful; act benevolently.

People can irritate me. Is there someone who annoys you? We should first, check to see if we are hungry, angry, lonely, or tired. The acrostic HALT is a good barometer for judging feelings. If my body is rested and well fed, I examine myself to see what causes the offense to my spirit. I ask myself, *Why does this person aggravate me?* I usually find that it's a lack of love. Either I am not accepting God's love toward me, or I am not applying his love toward the one I feel contempt. The anxiety or irritation is also good barometer. I compare my emotion to the truth found in Scripture. When I knew I was unloving, I prayed for help to adjust my attitude. *Lord help me see this person as you do, and help him to know how much you love him.*

Only through the strength of the Spirit can we do the following, especially when we've been wronged.

Bears: *stegō*: to cover with silence; suffer; hide; conceal.

Hope: *elpizō*: expect; to trust in.

Endure: *hypomenō*: to remain i.e. abide; not recede; or flee, persevere.

When wronged, love leaves the consequences in God's hands. We are confident in God's judgment. We persevere, not holding a grudge, anger, or animosity toward the person who offended us.

Strength: *exischyō*: full strength; be entirely competent.

Comprehend: *katalambanō*: take eagerly; seize; possess; perceive.

God gives us the power to seize his love and apply it to ourselves and others.

Breadth: *platos*: suggesting great extent.

Surpasses: *hyperballō*: to throw beyond the usual mark; exceeding; excel.

Filled: *plēroō*: to cause to abound; to furnish or supply liberally.

His love is immeasurable. He cannot love us more or less than he does right now.

Discernment: *aisthēsis*: perception; judgment.

To have delicate discernment is difficult at times. We judge the situation. This does not mean we render a guilty verdict. To judge means to weigh in the balance, to take all the facts and compare them to the Word of God.

I was convicted by Philippians 1:9-10 NIV when I needed wisdom for a situation with a friend.

And this is my prayer: that your love may abound more and more in knowledge and depth of insight, so that you can discern what is best, that you may be pure and blameless for the day of Christ,"

My good friend Lisa introduced me to Mary. Mary lived close to me and we became fast friends. One day Lisa called me.

"She needs you to back off. She knows what she's doing. She's too afraid to say anything to you. She loves you and does not want to hurt your feelings," Lisa hesitantly said to me as we discussed our mutual friend, Mary, and the upcoming Christmas party. My heart broke. We decided to plan a Christmas get together at Mary's house. She was eager for me to help. Little did I know, she orchestrated this event each year; it was the highlight of the Christmas season for many. I am a zealous party planner. I wanted to please my new friend and carry my load, so I called her to offer ideas and assistance, after all, she asked for my help. The next Sunday we spoke after church. The following week I called to say hi and discuss the details of the upcoming party. She seemed hesitant about my ideas and cut our conversation short. I was confused.

Are we planning this together? I thought to myself.

After my phone conversation with Lisa, I realized my motive was to be admired and not thought of as a slouch. I didn't inquire about Mary's talents and abilities. I longed to show off mine.

I found my Bible. Through tears of repentance I read Philippians 1:9–11.

As I prayed for delicate discernment in all situations, especially with Mary, God gave me the wisdom to call her and apologize. She apologized for confiding in Lisa and not speaking with me first. The party was wonderful. We sang Christmas carols, ate great food, and thanked God for Jesus. Mary and I are still great friends. Lisa too.

The evil one would love us to remain in the unspoken hurt and pain by putting an unseen wall between us.

When love meets discernment, the fruit of God's glory and righteousness is revealed. That is why surgical prayer is so important. It works. Even for the vilest offense.

The truth is, God cares for each soul, even the one so deep in darkness there seems to be no way out.

God's radical change in my heart has me praying for the souls of murderers, thieves, and child molesters. (Now that's radical.)

People rejoiced when an inmate named Jeffery Dahmer was murdered in prison.

"He is going to burn in hell for what he did," a friend said.

"That animal deserves to die," another friend echoed.

Jeffrey Dahmer committed the most heinous crimes. He is known as the Milwaukee Cannibal. Dahmer was a serial killer and sex offender who committed the rape, murder, and dismemberment of seventeen men and boys between 1978 and 1991. I prayed for his soul. Little did I know, a member of the local church in Oklahoma, was contacted by the prison to perform a baptism on Dahmer. Why such a change in heart from this madman? While in prison, Dahmer studied the Bible, repented of his sins, and was baptized. Dahmer continued to study the Bible for a few months before a fellow inmate murdered him.

The apostle Paul, before he was saved, hunted Christians. He had them thrown in jail or stoned to death: "But Saul, still breathing threats and murder against the disciples of the Lord, went to the high priest and asked him for letters to the synagogues at Damascus, so that if he found any belonging to the Way, men, or women, he might bring them bound to Jerusalem" (Acts 9:1–2).

God's love captured his heart and replaced it with a desire to serve the ones he once despised.

Paul wrote most of the New Testament. Some of his letters were written from prison.

No soul is beyond the reach of God's saving love. Jesus said, "But I say to you, Love your enemies and pray for those who persecute you" (Matthew 5:44).

Will you join me in praying for the wicked, lost, and downcast? Praying for them does not mean we agree with their sin. It means we trust the one who died for that sin. The sin that ultimately separates us from God is rejecting the free gift of eternal life through Christ Jesus.

Ultimate love is wanting even the vilest sinner to repent and have the hope of eternal life.

The theme throughout all of Paul's prayers is to know Christ intimately—to know his love for us and the power we have in the Holy Spirit. Let's pray the surgical prayer for our brothers and sisters as we pray for ourselves. Let us pray for the wicked who perform their deeds in the dark. May the light of God's love penetrate their hard rock hearts and turn it toward their maker.

Many things can keep us from accepting this love. In Romans 8:37–39, Paul, the murderer-turned-child-of-God states, "No, in all these things we are more than conquerors through him who loved us. For I am sure that neither death nor life, nor angels nor rulers, nor things present nor things to come, nor powers, nor height nor depth, nor anything else in all creation, will be able to separate us from the love of God in Christ Jesus our Lord."

Praying the surgical prayer will produce supernatural results. It's not a formula; it's a conversation with the only one who can perform spiritual surgery in us and others, so that the light of Christ will be known to the world—the light that changes our whine to shine.

============================

Memory verse
Acts 6:4, "But we will devote ourselves to prayer and to the ministry of the word."

Light reflection questions

1. How often do you pray?

2. What part of the surgical prayer stood out to you?

3. Should we pray for our enemies? Explain.

Praying the Armor

Nightmares can cause us to wake with a scream in our throat. I had many horrible dreams. One of the worst: being naked on stage and everyone laughing at me. I shudder at the thought of it ever happening in real life. I walked around spiritually naked. My soul and mind vulnerable to all of Satan's attacks, until I learned to cloth myself with the armor of God.

We are all defenseless without praying and donning the armor of God. We must recognize we are in a battle. That battle is won through prayer and the Word.

Demons shiver when we storm the gates of heaven, sword in hand. The evil one regurgitates at the proclamation of God's Word. He cowers, knowing that he is defeated. The Word has that kind of power, so we must have an attitude of prayer during this battle we call life. Scripture should be in our heart and on our tongue.

Satan preys on those who are unarmed for the battle—those who do not realize the war has been won. Satan's motive? He renders believers paralyzed and too afraid or weak to obey their Master. He wages war against his enemy (us) with lies. When Satan preys, we pray! Praying the truth of the Word is spiritual warfare. I see it firsthand as I pray for myself and others, especially when I pray Scripture and claim the promises of God.

We must equip ourselves for this warfare like soldiers equip themselves for battle. We must always be prepared by putting on the full armor of God.

My father-in-law, Joseph J. Bisbano Jr. reminded me of the importance of preparation when he shared this story. He was a machinist's mate first class and acting chief of the USS Lavallette during World War II.

"There was nothing in sight anywhere except for a few shark fins circling the raft at about five hundred feet away." I listened in amazement as my father-in-law shared the heart-wrenching account of the torpedoing of the USS Lavallette in the Coral Sea during the Battle of Guadalcanal.

"The Lavallette was smoke screening the USS Chicago (a heavy cruiser) when it was attacked by dive-bombers and torpedo planes. I was assigned to the after-engine room and had left to go the galley for a fresh pitcher of water when the torpedo hit. There was a brilliant flash, followed by a loud rumble and an onrush of heated air that was breathtaking." I was mesmerized as this brave sailor, now in his eighties, and how he recalled the story like it was yesterday. Tears fill my eyes as he shared how he dove into the oil-slicked waters, held his breath, found a safe place to surface, and was rescued by his shipmates who floated on a raft. There were about fifty men, some injured. The uninjured took turns hanging over the side because there was not enough room in the raft for all the men.

"I wore my shark repellent all the time; I did not think I would need it, but like a good soldier, I was always dressed for battle."

What this gallant man told me next sent chills down my spine.

"I saw my brothers eaten by sharks as they hung over the side of the raft because they did not wear their repellent." A tear filled his eye as he shook his head. "If only they listened to their training and put on everything they needed, they would be alive today."

This horrific account made me think of the spiritual application. We are in a spiritual battle. Our enemy circles us like a savage animal waiting to devour us: "Be sober-minded; be watchful. Your adversary the devil prowls around like a roaring lion, seeking someone to devour" (1 Peter 5:8).

Ephesians 6 commands us to prepare for battle and put on the full armor of God. We must put on our armor, not rely on another person to dress us spiritually.

I think of young David when he went to King Saul to announce that he would fight the giant Goliath. King Saul tried to put his armor on David to protect the boy. It did not fit.

David knew, as everyone coward around him, who would protect him and fight the battle on his behalf: "The Lord who delivered me from the paw of the lion and the paw of the bear will deliver me from the hand of this Philistine" (1 Samuel 17:37).

As David faced the giant, he proclaimed, "You come against me with sword and spear and javelin, but I come against you in the name of the Lord of hosts, the God of the armies of Israel" (1 Samuel 17:45).

Our armor is Jesus Christ. We pray to acknowledge that we are in Christ. He is our protection.

For as many of you as were baptized into Christ have put on Christ. (Galatians 3:27)

But put on the Lord Jesus Christ. (Romans 13:14)

We are in Christ. He is our shield and great reward, and our only offensive weapon is the Word of God. John 1:1 states, "In the beginning was the Word, and the Word was with God, and the Word was God." The more we know the Word, the more we know Jesus because he is the Word. This knowledge will make our spiritual armor impenetrable.

Warn your brothers and sisters, especially those closer to the battle lines or outside the raft. They must be fully prepared.

My father-in-law returned home, raised a beautiful family, and became a pillar of courage and integrity. As a praying man, he was always prepared for battle.

We have enemies. We cannot deny it or sweep it under the rug. The most powerful weapon our enemy has against us is making us think he does not exist or he uses half-truths to deceive us.

In the garden of Eden, the serpent said to Eve, "Did God actually say . . . ?" He confused Eve and made her doubt, causing eternal consequences for mankind.

Praying the armor of God is one of the most important prayers any believer can pray. We are in a spiritual battle, and if we do not put on the armor, we will be wounded and left for dead. A soldier puts on armor and protection before the battle; we must do the same. We are in a spiritual battle. We don't want to be a casualty of war.

Finally, be strong in the Lord and in his might. Put on the whole armor of God, that you may be able to stand against the schemes of the devil. For we do not wrestle against flesh and blood, but against the rulers, against the authorities, against the cosmic powers over this present darkness, against the spiritual forces of evil in the heavenly places. (Ephesians 6:10–12)

For though we live in the world we do not wage war as the world does. (2 Corinthians 10:3 NIV)

Be alert and of sober mind. Your enemy the devil prowls around like a roaring lion looking for someone to devour. (1 Peter 5:8 NIV)

The Word states we fight the battle in more than one place—earth and the heavenly realm. We cannot say we did not heed the warning.

So, what are the pieces of armor we need to put on so we are not spiritually naked? Ephesians 6:14–17 NIV says, "Stand firm then, with the belt of truth buckled around your waist, with the breastplate of righteousness in place, and with your feet fitted with the readiness [sandals] come from the gospel of peace. In addition to all this, take up the shield of faith, with which you can extinguish all the flaming arrows of the evil one. Take the helmet of salvation and the sword of the Spirit, which is the word of God."

Paul wrote this portion of Scripture from prison. He saw the armor the Roman guards donned for battle and applied the physical armor to spiritual armor. Each piece of armor is for a specific reason and must be worn for complete protection.

People dress in different ways. Some put their pants on first, then a shirt, or vice versa. In each case, people leave their house fully dressed, we hope. It is the same for the armor of God. As long as we are wearing it, the order in which we don it doesn't matter. For me, it is easier to start at the top of the head and work my way to my feet and finish with a sword and shield. I wrote a song for my son so he would remember to be spiritually dressed: "Put on the helmet of salvation and the breastplate of righteousness. I'm almost dressed! The belt of truth. The sandals of peace. Take up my shield of faith and my sword. Now I'm dressed in the Lord. YEAH!"

He loves it! I taught this song at ladies' retreats. What fun to see a bunch of grown women putting their hands on their head, beating their chest, touching their waist, and traveling to their toes! We all giggle as we hold the shield in front of us and swing the sword of the Word. I call it armor aerobics! We may look silly, but it's a great way to get ready for battle. Each part is important. Let's examine each piece.

Helmet of Salvation

Satan wants us to doubt our salvation and the complete work of Christ at the cross. The helmet protects our minds against discouragement, the desire to give up, or the lies causing us to waver. The helmet secures our hope with the knowledge we are saved.

We demolish arguments and every pretension that set itself up against the knowledge of God, and we take captive every thought to make it obedient to Christ. (2 Corinthians 10:5 NIV)

Breastplate of Righteousness

Satan attacks our hearts and minds. The words "heart" and "mind" are often interchangeable in the Bible. His battle plan is to attack the seat of our emotions rendering us feeling unworthy and hopeless. We begin to distrust God and the truth of his Word. Living by emotion is dangerous. If our feelings go unchecked against the truth of the Word, or we run after the emotion, we are exposed to all the temptations of Satan and become easy prey to the enemy. We must stand firm in the righteousness of Christ!

He put on righteousness as a breastplate, and a helmet of salvation on his head. (Isaiah 59:17)

But since we belong to the day, let us be sober, putting on faith and love as a breastplate, and the hope of salvation as a helmet. (1 Thessalonians 5:8 NIV)

Belt of Truth

Truth is represented as a belt, which protects our abdomen and gathers our garments so we can fight effectively! The belt played a crucial role in the success of a soldier's armor. It held the scabbard, without which there would be no place to put a sword. The sword, the Word, is our only offensive weapon against the Devil. He fights with lies. He is called the father of lies. He whispers them into our ears. *You are ugly. You are weak. Did God really say . . . ?* Only the truth can set us free and fight the lies. Remember, Jesus said, "Your Word is truth." (John 17:17) Speaking of himself he said, "I am the Way the Truth and the Life." (John 14:6)

Righteousness will be his belt and faithfulness the sash around his waist. (Isaiah 11:5 NIV)

Speaking of Satan, " He was a murderer from the beginning, and does not stand in the truth, because there is no truth in him. When he lies, he speaks out of his own character, for he is a liar and the father of lies." (John 8:44).

Footgear

The footgear is often called the sandals of peace/gospel. It is the readiness to spread the good news of salvation. Satan wants us to think telling others the good news is worthless and futile. He wants us to believe the task is too big, and we are not capable. The Romans' footgear usually had three-inch spikes on the bottom so they could stand their ground and remain balanced. The spiritual footgear gives us the motivation to be obedient to the Lord and proclaim his salvation while remaining steadfast.

Shield of Faith
The shield of faith protects us from Satan's fiery arrows. In a physical battle, fiery arrows were launched at the beginning of an attack. The purpose was not only to injure the enemy but to confuse and panic the enemy. The attacks from Satan can be in the form of setbacks, insults, depression, a sense of panic, and temptation. The shield Paul describes is a large, oblong shield that would protect the whole body, not the small round one. The stronger our shield, the stronger our faith.

Sword
The only offensive weapon. The sword is the Word of God. The sword used by Roman soldiers was smaller and used for close combat. Soldiers trained hard for the battle. We must memorize the Word so we will be able to use it effectively. We must train our brain for the fight. A great example is when Jesus combated the temptation of Satan in the wilderness. To temptation Jesus replied, "It is written!"

> For the word of God is living and active. Sharper than any double-edged sword, it penetrates even to dividing soul and spirit, joints, and marrow; it judges the thoughts and attitudes of the heart. (Hebrews 4:12)

> Out of his mouth comes a sharp sword with which to strike down the nations. He will rule them with an iron scepter. He treads the winepress of the fury of the wrath of God Almighty! (Revelation 19:15)

A mighty warrior, fit for battle, must pray the armor, which is the Lord Jesus Christ.

Besides this you know the time, that the hour has come for you to wake from sleep. For salvation is nearer to us now than when we first believed The night is far gone; the day is at hand. So then let us cast off the works of darkness and put on the armor of light. Let us walk properly as in the daytime, not in orgies and drunkenness, not in sexual immorality and sensuality, not in quarreling and jealousy. But put on the Lord Jesus Christ, and make no provision for the flesh, to gratify its desires. (Romans 13:11–14)

We must cast off the works of darkness and put on the armor of light like we take off or put on clothes. Therefore, every day, put on the Lord Jesus Christ! When we put on Christ, we put on all the armor of God and stand equipped to both defend and attack.

My friend Connie Wohlford explains the need for wearing the armor at home, "We need to recognize demonic influence and activity even within the walls of our homes. We must put on the whole armor and war against wickedness and darkness that rises up against our spouse, ourselves, our parents and our children. . . . We may take off our clothes at the end of the day, but we should never remove our armor, perhaps especially at home."

Notice the word "stand" is used three times in this segment of Scripture. God fights the battle for us as we proclaim his Word or sword. We cannot run or try to fight the evil one in our power. Satan can be deceptive and lead us astray. That is why we stand firm.

"And no wonder, for even Satan disguises himself as an angel of light." (2 Corinthians 11:14)

Let us put on the Light of the World and extinguish the lies of Satan. Remember, we have victory in Jesus already. Light reveals darkness and sin so we can eradicate it through prayer and the Word. We are overcomers with great promises.

"[T]he word of God abides in you, and you have overcome the evil one." (1 John 2:14)

"They will fight against you, but they shall not prevail against you, for I am with you, declares the LORD, to deliver you." (Jeremiah 1:19)

Prayer is powerful. It allows us to communicate with our Creator, Father, and friend. Prayer protects us from the evil one who wants to destroy us. Also, God hears the prayers of his children and desires to answer them. He specifically teaches us how to pray. He even prays for us when we do not know what to pray: " In the same way the Spirit also helps our weakness; for we do not know how to pray as we should, but the Spirit Himself intercedes for us with groanings too deep for words; 27and He who searches the hearts knows what the mind of the Spirit is, because He intercedes for the saints according to the will of God." (Romans 8:26–27).

Prayer is not magic. We do not release God's power by saying words in the correct order.

We must acknowledge that God fights the battle.

James 4:7 says, "Submit to God resist the Devil."

I encourage you to research more prayers in the Bible. Memorize them and pray them for yourself and others. Don't let the demons see you naked. Get spiritually dressed!

We need prayer especially when we go through times of trials and temptation. The prophets found themselves in times of trial and called to God, and we can too!

Now that we know how to pray, let's learn why we go through these trials and tribulations.

===========================

Memory verse
Romans 13:12, "The night is far gone; the day is at hand. So then let us cast off the works of darkness and put on the armor of light."

Light reflection questions:

1. Why do we don the armor of God?

2. Who is our enemy?

3. Which piece of the armor resonates with you during the battle? Explain.

R: Refined to Shine

"Blows that wound cleanse away evil; strokes
make clean the innermost parts." (Proverbs
20:30).

Expect Trials

Horrendous acts of evil occur each day. I don't have to
read the paper to encounter news of violence. I look
at the life of a close friend who loves Jesus. This friend
and her family endured the brutal murder of a loved one, a
deadly car accident, cancer, robbery, death threats, and prodigal children. She is a believer, yet she still asks, "Where is God?
Why does he allow this to happen?"

I hear these questions and others like them from both believers and nonbelievers.

"I cannot believe in a God who says he is love and allows the
murder of innocent children. Look what happened in Sandy
Hook. Why didn't your God save those children?"

"Why does God let evil people live?"

"Why did the drunk driver live and my daddy have to die?"

"Why is God silent when there is so much suffering?"

What do I tell them when I also ask similar questions of God?

God does not mind his children asking questions. He welcomes the questions because his Word contains the answers.
Some of the answers are difficult to understand or accept, but
as we will see in the Word, trials and temptations are inevitable. People choose to sin, which affects the lives of others. We
also live in a world filled with the effects of original sin, causing

disease and aging. We also have an enemy who prowls around trying to devour us and causing us to sin against others and God.

The question we must ask first concerns the root of our suffering. Is the suffering the effect of sin from the world, a scheme of Satan, or is it a self-inflicted fleshly desire? It will be profitable for us to break each of these into separate categories so we can have a better understanding of what type of trial we are enduring, and we will better know how to fight it. As I stated in the introduction to our journey, there will be many Bible verses. The Word will change our attitudes toward sin and give us a realistic look at the truth.

One word for sin in the New Testament is *hamartanō*, which means to miss or wander from the path of uprightness and honor; to do or go wrong; to violate God's law, trespass, offend, or miss the mark (and so not share in the prize). The word is also an archery term.

In the olden days, people played an archery game called Saints and Sinners. There was a hoop at the top of a pole, and the men had to shoot their ten arrows through the hoop. They were called a saint if they got all ten arrows through the hoop. If they missed only one, they were called a sinner. Yes, it's possible to be a sinner even if we hit the mark the majority of the time. We don't get points for trying hard and missing the mark. Ultimately, we will all miss the mark at least once. This is why Jesus came to earth to die for ALL sin.

The apostle Paul placed sin into three categories: "And you were dead in the trespasses and sins in which you once walked, following the course of this world, following the prince of the power of the air, the spirit that is now at work in the sons of disobedience—among whom we all once lived in the passions of our flesh, carrying out the desires of the body and the mind, and were by nature children of wrath, like the rest of mankind" (Ephesians 2:1–3).

The world, the flesh, and the devil wage war against us. Even though we are dead to sin and alive in Christ, old thought patterns are still there and they must be changed. Here are some examples.

"If I'm good, good things will happen to me."

"A loving God would not allow this to happen."

"This sin isn't that bad."

"I deserve fame and fortune."

When we remain in our old way of thinking, we give power to the flesh, the world, and Satan. If you struggle with the old way of thinking, please review the principle of transforming the mind with the Word.

The breakdown:

World: refers to the ungodly culture and society that opposes the Lord. Materialism and the desire for immediate gratification top the list.

Flesh: our fallen nature. The sinful longings for physical pleasure like sexual sin, alcohol, drugs, gluttony, pride, and so on.

Devil: Satan.

World: the riches and glories of the world still appeal to us, so we must maintain our guard lest we fall into bondage. Money and popularity aren't the enemy. However, we relinquish the throne to the world when we love fame and fortune more than God.

Many professing Christians drink of the well of worldly pleasures. Even musicians, speaker/teachers, and pastors get lured away by money and fame. Ultimately, they find themselves drowning in sin. If they don't turn to Christ and grab his hand, they may end up like the disciple, Judas Iscariot.

Deception slithered unnoticed through the disciples. But Jesus knew that Judas Iscariot would betray him. Jesus even washed Judas's feet on the night Judas betrayed his teacher with a kiss. Jesus gave Judas every chance to repent, but he did not. The silver gleamed in his eyes and changed his heart: "Then when Judas, his betrayer, saw that Jesus was condemned, he changed his mind and brought back the thirty pieces of silver to the chief priests and the elders, saying, "I have sinned by betraying innocent blood." They said, "What is that to us? See to it yourself." And throwing down the pieces of silver into the temple, he departed, and he went and hanged himself" (Matthew 27:3–5).

Judas confessed that he deceived innocent blood. His admission was not grief over what he did. Remorse is not repentance. Remorse is the illusion of righteousness. He did not repent and have godly sorrow that leads to salvation. Sorrow in and of itself doesn't produce anything except bad feelings, but godly sorrow leads to repentance—a change in both thinking and action. Judas tried to buy back his innocence by throwing the money into the temple. In the end, money could not soothe his conscience. He tried to redeem himself with his actions—a worldly solution to his spiritual problem.

For godly grief produces a repentance that leads to salvation without regret, whereas worldly grief produces death. (2 Corinthians 7:10)

Judas walked with the Savior, saw miracles, and carried the money purse, yet he betrayed the lover of his soul.

The Bible has a lot to say about the love of the world. Here is another verse that convicted me:

Do not love the world or the things in the world. If anyone loves the world, the love of the Father is not in him. (1 John 2:15)

We must guard ourselves against falling in love and obsessing over the world and the passions and pleasures it offers.

James 4:4 says, "[W]hoever wishes to be a friend of the world makes himself an enemy of God." I don't want to be an enemy of the one who saved me from eternal damnation by romancing the world. Do you?

Flesh: our sinful nature seeks to satisfy its lusts. Our desires can express themselves through our thoughts and actions in a way that opposes the spiritual nature. I experienced this firsthand.

I longed to have a man in my life. A relationship gave me security and self-worth. I thought, *Hey, if a guy wants me, I must be worth loving.* This carried over into my Christian life. As a new believer, I remained in a relationship with a great man; we will call him D. He was divorced and had two beautiful children. D. loved me, doted on me, and made me feel like a queen. Finally, a relationship where I felt unconditional love. D. was well respected in the community. Everyone told me he was a loving, kind gentleman. To top it off, he was from England, and his accent melted my heart. We worked together, and I watched how he treated others.

This guy's a keeper, I said to myself. He spent each waking hour with me if he was not working or with his children. He often had his children, and we all bonded. I dreamt of the day we would marry. His daughter, our flower girl, and his son, our ring bearer. I prayed and asked God to give me wisdom. During our dating time, his ex-wife would call and need him to do something for the kids. The calls became more frequent. I asked him if his wife wanted to get back together with him.

"Absolutely not."

"Please ask her," I said one day.

After six or seven times prodding him to ask her he finally did, and she said, "Not really."

I shared my heart with Kay, the associate pastor's wife. She gave me all the biblical advice:

"No sex; pray together; and ask him why they divorced."

I was confused. *Why does the reason for divorce matter?*

She must have read my mind.

"If there is any chance of reconciliation in their marriage, you need to sever all ties and allow God to reconcile them," Kay said as she guided me through the Bible verses on God, marriage, and divorce.

We prayed, and I left with a desire to do God's will. The battle between spirit and flesh raged in the members of my body. I ached to be with him, to marry him, to ignore the godly advice.

His ex doesn't want him back. She asked for the divorce, so we are free to marry, I tried to convince myself and God. I told him I wanted to please God and wait for marriage. He was perfectly fine with no sexual intimacy and wanted to rededicate his life to the Lord.

"I love you, Cherrilynn. I want us to work," D proclaimed.

See, Lord, he wants to do the right thing. His children love me. We can be together, right?

Wrong. The Holy Spirit was not a still, small voice at this moment. I knew what I had to do. I guess I knew it the entire time. God spoke to my heart and reiterated he wanted D. and his wife to reconcile, and I was standing in the way. The screams of the flesh soon turned into a whisper when I acknowledged that I was in a battle and must obey.

I sobbed as I told D. that God wanted him to get back together with his ex. He begged me not to go.

"How do you know God wants that? We love each other."

I walked away devastated yet trusting God.

He called many times, and I did not answer. He stood at my door crying hysterically. I did not let him in. The last words I spoke to him were through tears and a locked door.

"D., be with your wife. That's what God wants."

I quit my job and allowed my heart to heal. I felt a peace knowing I was obedient to God, but my heart broke.

I prayed for reconciliation in D.'s marriage. I prayed that they both would dedicate their lives and children to the Lord. Not quite the Hallmark ending I wanted, but obedience triumphs a Hallmark ending any day.

I began a new chapter in my life, working in a law office in Providence. I made new friends as I rode the bus to work each morning. God used me to shine my light into the lives of those around me.

Five years had passed. D. was a fond yet painful memory. One day as I waited for the bus, a familiar face approached me.

"I know you, but I cannot remember how," I said to the woman who now stood next to me.

"We worked together," she said. "My name is Mary."

"Yes, now I remember. You started working a few days before I left."

We chatted a bit, and I asked the question burning in my soul. "Is D. still there?"

My heart beat faster as I held my breath for the answer.

"No, he remarried his wife, and he and the kids moved back to England," Mary said.

"Yippee! I am so happy for him. He and I were good friends, and I told him he should get back together with his wife. God is so good. Is he happy?" I asked.

"Very. The family started attending church before they left. His face beamed every time he came to work."

Mary never knew the entire story.

My obedience overcame my flesh, and a marriage was saved. I guess there was a Hallmark ending after all.

The flesh still tries to rear its ugly head in my life, but it's a sin I must conquer to fully please the Lord. I must slay that dragon with the sword of the Word, as we discussed in the chapter on transforming your mind with the Word.

Devil: he is our adversary whose main purpose is to render us crippled in the battle. There's no room for pity parties or a "woe is me" attitude. Trust me, I have thrown many self-loathing parties. A victory party is more fun. People want to attend a victory party. Pity parties are a solo event.

We must be vigilant. Satan has been our enemy since the beginning of time. Remember, at the fall of man God said to the serpent (Satan): "I will put enmity between you and the woman, and between your offspring and her offspring he shall bruise your head, and you shall bruise his heel" (Genesis 3:15).

Jesus states in John 10:10, "The thief comes only to steal and kill and destroy. I came that they may have life and have it abundantly.

Peter the apostle warns us, "Be sober-minded; be watchful. Your adversary the devil prowls around like a roaring lion, seeking someone to devour" (1 Peter 5:8).

He knew the schemes of the devil. Jesus allowed Satan to sift Peter, and Peter came out shining. He did not let Satan have him for dinner.

I know I don't want to be a meal for the evil one. We have the power working in us to fight this battle. How do we get our names taken off Satan's snack menu?

We must learn of his strategies and teach others, especially our children, how to fight this spiritual battle. Reread the chapter on praying the armor if you need a refresher course.

Some of you may desire to close this book. Please don't. Battles are real and messy; we know God fights them for us as we stand firm.

One great tactic of our enemy is anonymity. He wants us to believe he doesn't exist or fighting him is sensationalism. Remember, he is a liar. He's also an angel of light coming in a form that appeals to us.

Satan also sends his minions, fallen angels, to possess and oppress humans. There are accounts in the Bible of demon possession. Believers cannot be demon-possessed, but we can experience oppression when we give the devil a foothold in our lives through sin and disobedience.

I taught my son how to fight the spiritual battle. He struggles with Asperger's and Attention Deficit Hyperactivity Disorder, (ADHD). He has endured many losses, and his heart is fragile. I won't go into detail. The story is my son's to tell. However, the presence of the evil one was palatable. He wanted to consume my son with thoughts of suicide and guilt. At times, my son became unruly and almost unrecognizable in his behavior. He was violent. This behavior progressed over a few months. Some of this behavior was due to his inability to understand his feelings and convey them. He would get frustrated and impatient with himself and others. He did not want to use the strategies we put in place to help him. That was the evil one's foothold.

One day was different. If you have a child with Asperger's, you understand the times of violent outburst. He bit me and screamed as he exploded into rage. There was a distant look about my son. I held him while he tried to bite me. I felt a gloomy weight of darkness over the both of us. I knew this was more than a familiar episode. I claimed the blood of Christ and said, "Satan you must leave. We are children of God, and you have no power over us. Lord, please intervene."

The dark cloud lifted; peace came over my son. My son is not possessed. He accepted the free gift of eternal life when he was four years old. However, there was oppression.

The vile oppression lasted a month. Each time we claimed the blood of Christ, stood firm, and asked God to intervene. The evil oppression finally left, so we thought.

One day my son was in his room reading. He became agitated. As I stood in the kitchen, I heard him proclaim, "Behind me, Satan. You have no power over me. I am a child of God. Lord help me!"

I ran into his room and hugged him. He said, "Mom, that evil guy tried to get me again, so I had to sic Jesus on him."

We began to play praise and worship music in my son's room throughout the night. The evil spirit left. We continue to have the radio on a worship station while my son sleeps peacefully.

Not everyone experiences Satan with such force. You may not even believe this happens. However, the apostle Paul himself stated, "[A] thorn was given me in the flesh, a messenger of Satan to harass me, to keep me from becoming conceited" (2 Corinthians 12:7).

Many try to expound on the word "thorn" by saying it was Paul's eyes, epilepsy, or something else. The Scripture states it was "a messenger of Satan." Paul was harassed by a demonic spirit. The Bible does not state specifically what the thorn in the flesh was, so I will not try to guess. Personally, I say, let the Scripture speak for itself.

Satan probably jumped at God's permission to afflict Paul, but God had a purpose and allowed Satan's messenger to successfully keep Paul from conceit, and God was glorified in the affliction. The thorn was given to Paul, and God allowed it like he allowed Satan to tempt Job.

If you have not had the opportunity to study the book of Job, I highly recommend it, especially if you are going through a trial. Job said, "Though he slay me, I will hope in him" (Job 13:15).

Job endured the loss of his livestock, children, slaves, and property; only his wife and a few servants remained. God in his omniscience knew Job would remain faithful throughout the trials and tribulations. We can too because we have the Holy Spirit's power living in us.

* * *

Persecution is a form of trials and tribulations. It's unique. Christians are persecuted for believing in Jesus. Other trials and tribulation may have nothing to do with proclaiming faith in Christ. " Indeed, all who desire to live a godly life in Christ Jesus will be persecuted." (2 Timothy 3:12).

"Remember the word that I said to you: 'A servant is not greater than his master.' If they persecuted me, they will also persecute you. If they kept my word, they will also keep yours." (John 15:20)

The truth so important that God declares it many times in his Word.

So that no one would be unsettled by these trials, you know quite well that we were destined for them. In fact, when we were with you, we kept telling you that we would be persecuted. and it turned out that way, as you well know. (1 Thessalonians 3:3–4 NIV)

[S]trengthening the disciples and encouraging them to remain true to the faith. We must go through many hardships to enter the kingdom of God. (Acts 14:22 NIV)

Blessed are those who are persecuted because of righteousness, for theirs is the kingdom of heaven. Blessed are you when people insult you, persecute you and falsely say all kinds of evil against you because of me. Rejoice and be glad because great is your reward in heaven, for in the same way, they persecuted the prophets who were before you." (Matthew 5:10–12 NIV)

"Blows that wound cleanse away evil; strokes make clean the innermost parts." (Proverbs 20:30)

We know Christ endured intense suffering. We can learn endurance from him.

Although he was a son, he learned obedience from what he suffered. (Hebrews 5:8)

Jesus did not pass from disobedience to obedience. Jesus did not learn how to obey. He learned what it takes to be obedient amidst trials and persecution, so we can learn from him. If suffering was fit to teach the Son of God, we should welcome it as a tool of instruction in our lives. If trials are a part of life, let's choose to learn from them. No one likes to go through the refiner's fire. Jesus did not like it either. He cried to the Father, "Father, if you are willing, remove this cup from me. Nevertheless, not my will, but yours, be done."" (Luke 22:42).

However, he was obedient even unto death. God may not call us to death, but we must remind ourselves daily that we live in a world filled with sin and the results of sin. Believers and nonbelievers alike suffer from the result of a fallen world. The difference between children of God and nonbelievers is we can remain victorious in the world. We overcome by the power of the Spirit. We can shine brightly in this dark world: " The light shines in the darkness, and the darkness has not overcome it." (John 1:5).

We do not need to be governed by the evil of others or our circumstances. God is our vindicator, and we don't have to be evil. We overcome evil with good. Let love triumph over the enemy's hostility.

[T]hen the Lord knows how to rescue the godly from trials, and to keep the unrighteous under punishment until the day of judgment. (2 Peter 2:9)

Victory may not be imminent. Our enemy will not always repent or return our gestures of love. Jesus was rejected by one of the thieves on the cross, Judas, the centurion, and thousands of others who refused his free gift of eternal life. However, God promises we are overcomers and will see victory. If not on earth, in heaven.

"For everyone who has been born of God overcomes the world. And this is the victory that has overcome the world—our faith. 5Who is it that overcomes the world except the one who believes that Jesus is the Son of God?" (1 John 5:4–5)

Sometimes you love your enemies and they kill you. Many martyrs have proclaimed the Word of God to violent men only to be speared, beheaded, or burned at the stake. They had the victory even in death. We can too. Your life of love and obedience overcomes hostility. Either people repent, or they continue in sin and God takes vengeance.

Holy men in the Bible endured trials, temptations, and persecution.

The prophet Jeremiah warned the people of their disobedience. They did not listen. The Word of God burned in Jeremiah's bones; he made desperate attempts to turn the heart of the people back to their God. God allowed the enemy to ravish and conquer the land, leaving devastation and death. Jeremiah laments after seeing the destruction, his heart still longing to please God: "I am the man who has seen affliction by the rod of the LORD's wrath. He has driven me away and made me walk in darkness rather than light; indeed, he has turned his hand against me again and again, all day long" (Lamentations 3:1–3).

Jeremiah knew God and trusted God was present, even in desolation.

The steadfast love of the Lord never ceases; his mercies never come to an end; they are new every morning; great is your faithfulness. "The Lord is my portion," says my soul, "therefore I will hope in him." (Lamentations 3:22–24)

In our times of uncertainty during persecution and trials, let's learn from Jeremiah.

Jesus was also persecuted. "Remember the word that I said to you: 'A servant is not greater than his master.' If they persecuted me, they will also persecute you. If they kept my word, they will also keep yours." (John 15:20).

Paul was persecuted. "But we have this treasure in jars of clay to show this all-surpassing power is from God and not from us. We are hard pressed on every side, but not crushed; perplexed, but not in despair; persecuted, but not abandoned; struck down, but not destroyed. We always carry around in our body the death of Jesus, so that the life of Jesus may also be revealed in our body . . . for our light and momentary troubles are achieving for us an eternal glory that far outweighs them all" (2 Corinthians 4:7–9, 17 NIV).

My friend described this verse to me as a scale. Our troubles are on one side of the scale weighing it down and nothing tangible could be put on the other side to offset the weight. Nothing natural can help because it feels so heavy. Suddenly the glory of God appears, and with a delicate touch of his loving hand, the Father of mercy gently places his finger on the empty tray opposite the tray filled with our troubles. The troubles become light as feathers in the light of his glory and grace—the glory we get to bask in when we meet him face to face.

When we are consumed with trials and tribulations, God is the only one who can help. He tells us to cast our cares upon him. Life will not be easy. We must accept the fact and move on in the power of the Holy Spirit. Paul talks about this in Philippians 3:13–14, "But one thing I do: forgetting what lies behind and straining forward to what lies ahead, I press on toward the goal for the prize of the upward call of God in Christ Jesus."

Paul kept his eyes on the prize, Christ Jesus. This enabled him to learn contentment and endure during difficult times. He prayed for fellow believers: "I pray that your hearts will be flooded with light so that you can understand the confident hope he has given to those he called" (Ephesians 1:18 NLT).

We are called to shine our light in this dark world. We should expect to be led into the gloom so the light of his love can dissolve the dark places: "But their evil intentions will be exposed when the light shines on them" (Ephesians 5:13 NLT).

When evil intentions are exposed, revealing the truth of sin, some wayward souls may repent and turn to God. Without our light, they may not see God. Our light shines brightest in the dark. Even when evil and injustice plague our lives, we know God is there.

We must expect trials, tribulation, and persecution in life. Difficulties should propel us closer to our Lord. Blaming God gives our adversary joy and a foothold. We have a promise—eternity with no worries, tears, or pain. For now, let's go forth in the promise: "For this light momentary affliction is preparing for us an eternal weight of glory beyond all comparison" (2 Corinthians 4:17).

> You are the light of the world. A city set on a hill cannot be hidden. Nor do people light a lamp and

put it under a basket, but on a stand, and it gives light to all in the house. In the same way, let your light shine before others, so that they may see your good works and give glory to your Father who is in heaven. (Matthew 5:14–16)

Expect trials knowing that our God gives us the power to overcome. We are refined to shine if we allow difficult events to shape us into Christlikeness.

===========================

Memory verse
John 16:33, "In the world you will have tribulation. But take heart; I have overcome the world."

Light reflection questions:

1. How has the evil one deceived you?

2. What's the difference between persecution and trials/ tribulation?

3. What's the purpose of trials, tribulations, and persecution?

Refined to Shine

"Should we drive through the fire or wait until it burns out?" said Tom, the leader of our mission trip to Togo, West Africa.

"We have all the medical supplies. I say we drive," Pastor Mic Oke said. He was our translator.

Lord, keep us safe! I prayed.

I squeezed my husband's hand as our bodies slammed against the back of the seat. The van hurtled through the fire. "Though we go through the fire, we won't get burned!" we all said. I could barely hear anyone through the roar of the inferno.

The fire was so close I could hear the brush crackling around us. The heat was so severe that I felt its intensity through the metal of the van.

Seven seconds seemed like forever. Yes, I counted.

"Phew, we made it—just in time. The entire road is engulfed in flames," Tom said.

"I was afraid we were going to blow; this van has a gas leak," Pastor Mic said.

"Now you tell us!" we all said.

I looked back to see all the dead brush consumed, leaving the dark soil.

We asked Pastor Mic why the men were burning the land.

"Farmers use fire to return nutrients to the soil and to clear the ground of unwanted plants. We call it 'slash and burn.' Soon seeds will be planted, and the ground will yield lush green vegetation. It will supply food for the villages." I admired Pastor Mic. He was quick to teach us about Togo and its culture.

God uses fire as an analogy in Scripture. Fire burns away the impurities in metal and consumes anything not of value. Impurities plague our soul and the world around us—the result of sin.

Trials are a vehicle God uses to refine us and make us aware of our sin or the sin around us. Without the purifying process, we would remain dull and useless vessels in the service of the Lord. We are refined to shine.

"And I will put this third into the fire, and refine them as one refines silver, and test them as gold is tested. They will call upon my name, and I will answer them. I will say, 'They are my people'; and they will say, 'The LORD is my God.'" (Zechariah 13:9)

"Refinement" in the original language is *dokimazō*: to test; examine; prove; scrutinize (to see whether a thing is genuine or not), as metals; to deem worthy.

Charles Spurgeon, a well-known and highly respected nineteenth-century British preacher endured bouts of depression and gout. He stated, "If any of you, my hearers, are seeking the Lord at this time, I want you to understand what it means: you are seeking a fire which will test you, and consume much which has been dear to you. We are not to expect Christ to come and save us in our sins, he will come and save us from our sins; therefore, if you are enabled by faith to take Christ as a Savior, remember you take him as the purger and the purifier, for it is from sin he saves us."

We should expect trials. God purges us by removing sin and making us more like Christ. So, why does our blood boil when the heat intensifies?

I would throw a pity party and pout until I surrendered to the purging process.

Perfectionism needed purifying in this vessel. I drove my friends nuts. I belonged to a college and career group. We hiked, went to the beach, and studied the Word of God together.

One Sunday after church, the heat of the purification process intensified.

"Why don't the guys come with us anymore?" I said to my good friend.

My friend looked at the ground.

"What's wrong? Did I say something to offend them?" I said.

"The guys don't want to be around you because you're so controlling."

"Really it's because they are so indecisive." I felt hurt and needed to defend myself. Before my friend could say another word, I added, "No one can make a decision. We talk about it for hours, so I make the decision." *Did I really just say that? It sounded better in my head.*

"Cherrilynn, I have to be honest with you. You don't let anyone talk. You control the conversation. You make the decisions. You don't listen. That's why the guys haven't joined us the last few times we've gone out."

"I didn't realize. I feel so awful. Am I really that bad?"

"Yes, I love you and find you funny and smart, but in a group, you are very controlling. Is it because you were in the military?" My sweet friend tried to help me figure out why I bossed people around.

"Please pray for me. I don't want to chase people off because I'm controlling."

My friend hugged me. "God's got this, Cherrilynn."

Fear of the unknown and insecurities began to bubble up as I prayed and pondered my friend's statements. God used someone close to me to light the kiln and turn up the heat. I am forever grateful. I still have control issues. I recite the STAR principle to myself to see where the light is the dimmest.

Refinement is a continual process because sin is all around us and in us.

God is preparing us for something greater. We determined in the last chapter that trouble will invade our lives. Suffering is part of life—a part we wish we could eradicate. Until Christ returns, the effects of sin are inevitable. God, in his love and mercy, uses the thing that could separate us from him to make us more like him.

The apostle Peter understood this concept, "In this you rejoice, though now for a little while, if necessary, you have been grieved by various trials, so that the tested genuineness of your faith—more precious than gold that perishes though it is tested by fire—may be found to result in praise and glory and honor at the revelation of Jesus Christ" (1 Peter 1:6–7).

Peter mentions our great inheritance kept for us in heaven—that's why we rejoice. We don't rejoice because of the trial. We focus on heaven and the results of refinement.

When gold is placed in a red-hot furnace, the dross (anything that is not gold) is removed, and pure gold remains. God puts us in the furnace not to destroy us—he wants pure gold. Heat develops character. We need to be tested to prove our genuine pure faith.

"Feel the burn" is a statement made by athletes. Muscles must be exercised to be tested and strengthened. Continuous exercise induces sweat. Sweat removes toxins from the body. The body becomes healthier—ready to perform. No person runs a marathon without going through intense pain and preparation. A runner looks to the goal in spite of the agony.

One reason we lose perspective as we run the race of faith is that we look to our problem or situation and not to Christ. We forget we are destined to have adversity in our lives. We should be thankful God works everything, even difficulties, for our good, but it's hard to praise through the pain.

"Why does God allow you to writhe in pain? Can't he heal you?" my friend said.

"God will heal me of my fibromyalgia and chronic fatigue either here on earth or in heaven," I said.

"You suffer so much; I can't believe in a God that allows suffering."

I wanted to tell my friend about the glory God receives through my suffering. People are amazed at my joy—given by God. He uses the pain to purify me and keep me focused. In the past, I would say yes to everyone. "People pleaser" was a hat I wore daily. I ran myself ragged. I thought God wanted me to say yes to everything. I am his servant after all.

Fibromyalgia consumed my body. I had enough energy for a few tasks per day. The word "no" became a part of my vocabulary. I hated it. I felt like I let people down.

I found it difficult to rectify the pain and purification process until I sat at the feet of Jesus to glean from his life and teachings.

Suffering drove me to the throne room of God to seek wisdom, strength, and joy. In his presence is the fullness of joy. As I read the psalms, the Spirit spoke to me. God does not want me to do; he wants me to be. This verse gave me peace when my body ached: "Cease *striving* and know that I am God" (Psalm 46:10 NASB).

Most of us learn the verse, "Be still and know." (Psalm 46:10) But there is so much more to learn from these few words. The word "strive" resonates with me on a deeper level. With the words "be still," I picture myself as a kid trying to be still, fidgeting in my seat. I use every muscle to remain secured to my chair. The words "cease striving" evoke a picture of me resting in God's arms. I'm learning to cease striving. My body is feeling better, and the stress of people pleasing has subsided.

Complete understanding of the refinement process won't happen until we see him face to face. Meanwhile, we can ask God to give us the strength to endure the heat. We must remember that we are refined in the fire of trials to dissolve sin and prove our faith is genuine.

When the fiery trials try to consume us, let's choose not to let the evil of others or our circumstances render us useless. God is our vindicator, and we don't have to be evil. We overcome evil with good. Let love triumph over the enemy's hostility.

[T]he Lord knows how to rescue the godly from trials, and to keep the unrighteous under punishment until the day of judgment. (2 Peter 2:9)

Victory may not be imminent. Our enemy will not always repent or return our gestures of love. Jesus was rejected by one of the thieves crucified right next to him, Judas Iscariot, and thousands of others who refused his free gift of eternal life. However, God promises that we are overcomers and will see victory. If not on earth, in heaven. "For everyone who has been born of God overcomes the world. And this is the victory that has overcome the world—our faith. Who is it that overcomes the world except the one who believes that Jesus is the Son of God?" (1 John 5:4–5)

Jesus suffered the torment of crucifixion to obtain victory over death and sin. Let's shine and not whine so we can live in that victory even when it hurts.

* * *

Congratulations! We completed the final portion of *Shine, Don't Whine*. Trials are inevitable—that is a hard truth to swallow. When I acknowledged the effects of sin in this world are inevitable, my questions to God changed from "why God?" to "what will you teach me during this horrible time?" None of us like pain or heartache. God knows that we want to scream and mourn. He is with us through it, holding our hand and strengthening our faith. He does not want us to wallow in the pain; he wants us to gain from the pain.

Others watch and inquire as we endure hardship. I have seen hearts turn toward God as a friend endured cancer, all the while giving God the glory for sustaining her. She verbally praised him and placed her life in his hands. Her light amidst the pain pointed others to Jesus.

God carries my friend who lost her son in a rafting accident. She desperately misses him many years later. She knows she will see her son again when she gets to heaven. That promise gives her joy—meanwhile, her heart aches for the reunion. Many are attracted to her light, and she points them to Jesus.

God works even evil for our good. Does this amaze you too? Like Paul the apostle, we won't achieve contentment overnight. He learned it while he endured persecution, "Not that I am speaking of being in need, for I have learned in whatever situation I am to be content. . . . I can do all things through him who strengthens me" (Philippians 4:11, 13).

May we glorify our Father in heaven as we learn to endure trials, tribulations, and persecutions. May our light shine so bright in the darkness—pointing others to Jesus.

Our work is not over until we walk the streets of gold. The gospel message is the light we shine to others.

Will you join me in the next chapter to learn the importance of the good news and how to share it? Let's shine on.

============================

Memory verse

2 Corinthians 4:17–18, "For this light momentary affliction is preparing for us an eternal weight of glory beyond all comparison, as we look not to the things that are seen but to the things that are unseen."

Light reflection questions:

1. What is refinement?

2. Explain with Scripture why we go through trials.

3. How did Paul gain contentment?

Shine for Salvation

When I first began this journey, one of the Bible verses that inspired me was Daniel 12:3, "[T]hose who are wise will shine like the brightness of the heavens, and those who lead many to righteousness, like the stars forever and ever." I wanted to be wise and shine for the glory of God. I wanted to lead many to righteousness by telling them the good news about Jesus. The difficult part of sharing the message is that not everyone is open to the Creator's love.

The gospel message is not meant to be difficult, yet many miss the meaning because they are deep in their sin and refuse to let the light pierce the darkness. Others find it unobtainable due to self-hatred. Only God knows the heart of man. We are to be prepared to give a reason for the hope that is in us and leave the rest to God.

Jesus gave this call before he ascended into heaven, "Go into all the world and proclaim the gospel to the whole creation" (Mark 16:15). "Gospel" means "good news." Everyone wants to spread the good news, right? So why do we hesitate when the Spirit prompts us to speak? For me, I wasn't prepared, and I was afraid of rejection.

Think of when you first fell in love. Didn't you want to tell everyone about the person who consumed your every thought? The more I grew to love Jesus, the more I wanted to tell others what he did for me. I joined our missions team to learn how to share the gospel message. You don't need to join the missions team to learn how to share the good news. Scripture memorization is one way. Reading a gospel tract to the person is another.

As a new believer, I remember my exuberance to serve God. I was so thankful for a Father who accepted me. I was one of those annoying believers who told everyone they were going to hell if they did not repent and accept Christ. Have you met someone like me? Be gentle. If the Spirit leads you, explain that the love of God is not rude (1 Corinthians 13:5). I offended my family. Once I learned I was rude, I apologized.

"I'm sorry for being rude. I desire that you know Jesus. I don't apologize for what I said. I ask for forgiveness for the way I said it."

"You're forgiven. Now we'll let you visit more often," my stepdad said as he winked.

I received more invitations for dinner after I apologized.

No matter the method, God will use us. Rejection and ridicule are inevitable. However, there will be others who will rejoice because you took the time to learn the gospel message and share it with them. One gentleman was happy I listened to the Spirit.

I was joyful yet tired when I left the Blue Ridge Mountain Christian Writers Conference. I needed time to digest all the information I soaked up over the last few days.

Oh no, not my row, I said to myself as I watched a man with the physique of a linebacker walk toward me. The plane was small.

The large man sat shoulder to shoulder with me. For the next hour we squeezed into the back two seats of the puddle jumper.

He mumbled, "I don't want to talk if that is OK with you. So, what do you do?"

I was confused. He didn't want to converse but still asked me a question.

"I write."

"What do you write about?" he said as he tried to turn toward me, but his shoulders wouldn't move.

"I write mostly about the Bible.""

I felt his arm muscle tense.

I waited for him to excuse himself and sit in one of the many empty seats available. He remained.

"I went to church when I was little. My sister is still religious. She wants me to go back to church. I am on my way to see her."

Over the next thirty minutes, he shared. I listened.

"Our mom died a year ago. My sister and I mustered the courage to go to the house we grew up in. We want to face the memories together." He paused. I could see tears forming in his eyes as he changed the subject. "I work with many guys who hate God and make it known by their drinking, swearing, and sexual escapades. I don't want to be like them." He continued to talk.

I realized that guilt, pain, and uncertainty haunted him. He wanted peace of mind.

I prayed while he shared personal details of his life. I desired to share the love of Christ with him—only if the Spirit prompted me.

"I am so sorry about your mom. I will pray for you and your sister. God was my comfort when I lost my grandmother."

I could move my shoulder now; the tension in his shoulders released.

"Thank you so much. I do believe in God, ya know. I'm not a heathen," he stated.

The Spirit prompted me to be bold.

"We are all heathens apart from Jesus."

He tried to shift again to look at me.

"Really?" His mouth opened wider than his eyes.

The pilot's voice interrupted, "We are on our descent."

For the remaining few minutes, I explained. "Salvation is as easy as ABC."

A: acknowledge you are a sinner separated from God.

B: believe that Christ died for sin, rose again on the third day, and now sits at the right hand of the Father.

C: confess your sin, and cry out in repentance.

I recited Bible verses that corresponded to each letter and statement.

I concluded my rapid-fire statement as the wheels touched the pavement in Charlotte, North Carolina.

"Peace only comes from a relationship with your Maker," I said.

His entire countenance changed; he seemed lighter on his feet as he stood to grab his luggage from the overhead bin.

"Peace is what I desire."

The Lord was not finished with this man. I was the bold mouthpiece.

I looked up and fixed my eyes on his.

"The Lord is calling you. Today is the day of your salvation. We did not meet by chance. You must decide. It will be the most important decision you will ever make."

"I know," he said.

As we parted ways he said, "I can't wait to tell my sister about the unforgettable conversation we had."

"Tell her I'm praying for both of you as you go through your mom's things."

"Thank you. That means a lot. And thank you for taking the time to talk to me."

I don't know if he accepted the free gift of eternal life. That is in the hands of our mighty God. I praise God for the hour squeezed into that back row. I thank him for the boldness to speak to a man three times my size.

I consider it an honor to be used by God. He used prepared people in my life. I praise God for them and their boldness to give me the gospel. They took the time to learn how to present the precious gift of eternal life.

Our heavenly Father desires all his children to be prepared to give a reason for the hope that is in them. I was scared at first, but now I ask God to use me to share the good news.

I sometimes want to disobey when the Spirit prompts me to speak. I'm either too tired, too busy, or too intimidated.

When Paul the apostle preached, not everyone believed—still, he continued to speak the good news. His motivation? The knowledge that he was working with God.

We also work with God. God looks for a willing soul. Are you willing to work with God to shine your light into a dark world?

* * *

I attended a Christian counseling class to grow closer to God. The first task was to write our testimony so we could present it in one-, three-, and five-minute increments. This took time, but it was worth it. I minister to myself whenever I speak it. I encourage you to write your testimony. A testimony includes your life before salvation and after. My one-minute version was, "I was seeking the way to heaven. I showed up at a prayer meeting. The pastor showed me the way to heaven through Jesus. I now live for him. I have such peace and assurance of heaven." I'm smiling now, remembering the day of my salvation.

If people are interested in hearing more, I give them the ABCs of salvation.

Our testimony and the Word are vital to introducing others to Jesus—the lover of souls. "And they have conquered him [Satan] by the blood of the Lamb and by the word of their testimony" (Revelation 12:11).

I am grateful for Jesus and all he has done for me. I must tell others. I bet you want to also. Fear may creep in. "Will I know what to say? Will I say it right?"

Prayer and preparation are key.

A friend of mine told me she desperately wanted to share the gospel with a woman at work, and she prayed daily for an opportunity. The woman was hostile toward the gospel but would ask questions about the Bible. My friend would just answer the question because the Spirit stopped her from continuing the conversation. After a year of answering questions, the woman said to her, "Thank you for not trying to save me when I only wanted my questions answered. I think I'm ready to learn more about your Jesus."

God knows what a lost soul needs. We must pray and listen to the Spirit's prompting.

Preparation will also help us be more confident in our service to God. Memorizing Bible verses give us the tools to be used in a mighty way. The Word is what changes hearts.

Here are the verses I memorized for the ABC's of salvation.

A: acknowledge you're a sinner and separated from God. "[A]ll have sinned and fall short of the glory of God" (Romans 3:23).
B: believe that Christ died for your sin and that he is God. "[B]ut God shows his love for us in that while we were still sinners, Christ died for us" (Romans 5:8).
C: confess and cry out. "Because, if you confess with your mouth that Jesus is Lord and believe in your heart that God raised him from the dead, you will be saved." (Romans 10:9).

These are the verses I used for the giant on the plane. The living and active Word penetrated his soul. Only God knows if it changed him.

Our responsibility is to be obedient to the Spirit's instruction.

A group of people told me that if I didn't tell everyone about Jesus, people would go to hell. I walked around in fear—invading the privacy of anyone who would listen to me.

"If a house were burning down, you would run in and save the person—you have to tell everyone about Jesus, or they will burn in hell," a friend said to me.

We knocked on complete strangers' doors to impart our wisdom. My nose still hurts from all the doors slammed in my face.

My friend Karen and I looked for people to witness to one Halloween night. We were in Karen's car as we approached a group of teens.

"Do you know Jesus?" we asked.

"I do, but I don't know you," one boy responded as he walked away with all but one teen.

"If you were to die tonight, would you go to heaven," Karen asked the remaining girl.

Her eyes widened, and her mouth let out a scream as she ran away. "MOOOOOOM!!"

What were we thinking, approaching teens on Halloween? Our exuberance overshadowed wisdom. That girl probably thought we were going to kill her.

I had to rethink my witnessing approach.

Jesus said, "Go into all the world and proclaim the gospel to the whole creation. Whoever believes and is baptized will be saved, but whoever does not believe will be condemned" (Mark 16:15–16). I did not want people to be condemned, so I had to tell them. Right?

God's number one commandment was reiterated by Jesus, "You shall love the Lord your God with all your heart and with all your soul and with all your mind. This is the great and first commandment. And a second is like it: You shall love your neighbor as yourself" (Matthew 22:37–39). I was not loving God or others by being rude and obnoxious—acting out of fear. I repented.

I've since found a balance. I listen to the Spirit—he guides me. People will not go to hell because of me. I lose the joy and reward of being used by God to spread the good news.

We all can be a mouthpiece for God. Our light will shine in this dark world.

As children, we memorize our earthly ABCs. Will you join me in learning the spiritual ABCs? Rewards await. Let's ask God to lead us to one person so we can be wise and shine like a star.

================================

Memory verse
Daniel 12:3, "And those who are wise shall shine like the brightness of the sky above; and those who turn many to righteousness, like the stars forever and ever"

Light reflection questions:

1. Explain A in the salvation message.

2. Explain B in the salvation message.

3. Explain C in the salvation message.

Shine On

"In the same way, let your light shine before
others, so that they may see your good works
and give glory to your Father who is in heaven"
(Matthew 5:16).

Fearless Light

"Cherrilynn, I'm scared. This guy is getting too close to us."

My Navy friend and I enjoyed dinner and a late movie downtown. The bus stop was two blocks from the cinema.

"Just don't act scared. He may leave." I tried to reassure my friend.

We picked up our pace.

The stranger's footsteps grew louder and faster.

"He's getting closer!" she whispered

"Don't panic!"

"Cherrilynn, I'm scared."

With military precision, I did an about-face, looked the man in the eyes, and said "YOU ARE SCARING MY FRIEND. BACK OFF NOW!"

The man could not see my knees shake; I felt sick to my stomach.

His eyes widened as he felt my breath on his face.

"Sorry, I didn't realize I was so close," he said.

"Yeah, right! Pay attention next time; now leave!" I said trying to hold my weak legs in place, in awe of my sudden boldness (or stupidity).

The man turned around and walked in the opposite direction.

My friend and I ran to the bus stop. We vowed to bring the guys with us next time for protection.

If you're a child of God, you're being followed now!

Don't be scared; it's not a stranger but something so amazing—God's goodness and mercy. "Surely goodness and mercy shall follow me all the days of my life" (Psalm 23:6).

Psalm 23 depicts a glorious picture. In front of us, leading us, is Jesus, the Good Shepherd. He is the light of the world. He protects us and provides for our every need as we follow him.

Charles Surgeon, a pastor and theologian, describes this verse: "These twin guardian angels will always be with me at my back and my beck. Just as when great princes go abroad they must not go unattended, so it is with the believer."

As we walk in the light, God's goodness and mercy are behind us, protecting us.

Goodness: *tove*: beautiful, best, better, bountiful, cheerful, at ease.

Mercy: *checed*: favor, good deed, beauty, kindness.

We need not fear anything. However, we are still being refined, and the impurities—like fear, worry, doubt, and self-loathing—will rise to the surface. We must combat them with the Word. That is why I repeat many of the Bible verses in this book. They will become part of our being when we read them often.

Fear paralyzed me. I didn't want to disappoint God or others. As a new writer, I was catapulted into the literary world. My first job was writing a column for an online website. One month later I was asked to be the managing editor of that website. I knew nothing about uploading articles and graphics. The founder of the site, also a literary agent, believed in me and taught me the basics. I learned how to navigate the site and grew more confident.

One year into my job I became a submissions reader, responsible for forwarding book proposals to the agent. I sent pass letters to those that did not meet the requirements. I was fearful I would break someone's heart, and I prayed as I hit the send button. I also wore the hat of a junior literary agent. My knees shook, and my stomach jumped into my throat because I didn't want to fail God or my clients.

Now I own a business coaching writers from all over the world. The thought creeps in, *Will I fail? Do I really know what I'm doing?*

Fear of failure is not a new feeling. Life is filled with failure—school, relationships, jobs. I expect to fail, especially when I try something new.

As I read the Word of God, I learn I can overcome any obstacle because I have the power of Christ in me.

But I still wrestled with the lies of my past and the truth of the Word. The lies I believed were deeply rooted. The Word continues to penetrate my heart and destroys the lies.

God proves himself faithful over and over. God's power in me conquered the fear to speak, teach, write, and go places I never thought I could.

He led me to Honduras, Central America; Togo, Africa; the dark streets of the inner city, and unknown speaking platforms. The fear of failure was gone, or so I thought. God had another lesson for me.

People would tell me that I'm successful. I teach at writers' conferences, ladies' retreats, and small businesses and get accolades for my presentations. I try to always acknowledge that only God can enable me to accomplish these tasks. I committed this verse to memory. " His divine power has granted to us all things that pertain to life and godliness, through the knowledge of him who called us to his own glory and excellence." (2 Peter 1:3).

When I looked at what God was doing in and through me, I got frightened. I feared success.

Questions whirled through my head,

What if I don't want the spotlight on me?

What if someone in the audience confronts me with opposing views?

Will success make me prideful?

Will I fail God or someone I love?

I pondered these questions and realized that the fear of success is fear of failure wrapped in a pretty package of pride.

If I truly believe God's power works in and through me, how can I fail? If I operate in the Spirit and give God all the glory, fear should be eradicated, right?

[F]or God gave us a spirit not of fear but of power and love and self-control. (2 Timothy 1:7)

I can do all this through him who gives me strength. (Philippians 4:13 NIV)

Pride tried to control me again. When I ministered in my power, the fear returned. I looked to my inability and not to God's perfect ability in me. I put pleasing people ahead of pleasing God. I wanted man's acceptance more than I wanted to glorify my heavenly Father.

I demanded perfection from myself so I wouldn't fail God or people. When I did make a mistake, I beat myself up.

"Forgive me, Lord, for taking over again. Help me draw on your power."

I realized that my fear, no matter how pretty the package it's wrapped in, is distrust in God and his promises.

God has called each of us for a purpose, "For we are his workmanship, created in Christ Jesus for good works, which God prepared beforehand, that we should walk in them" (Ephesians 2:10).

He will help us accomplish the work he has ordained for us. God does not demand perfection, he desires a willing obedient heart.

I have the following verse hanging in my office to remind me that God empowers me; I need not fear failure or success: "Be strong and courageous and get to work. Don't be frightened by the size of the task, for the Lord my God is with you; he will not forsake you. He will see to it that everything is finished correctly" (1 Chronicles 28:20 TLB).

What has God called you to do? Are you frightened? Do you think he can't use you? God's light guides, and his grace and mercy are your protection. We have great hope.

The biblical account of Joshua conquering Jericho reveals a woman who was an outcast of society, used by men, and she needed a way out.

God wanted the Israelites to possess the land. Joshua, their leader, sent two spies to the city of Jericho to investigate.

They entered the home of Rahab, a prostitute. Imagine her reaction when two men of God approached her. I wonder if she felt fear and shame.

After the spies had entered Rahab's home, located in the city walls, the king of the city sent men to retrieve the spies. She hid the spies on her roof. She lied and told the men that the spies left. We continue the story right after the men left to pursue the spies in Joshua 2:8–21.

> Before the men lay down, she came up to them on the roof and said to the men, "I know that the Lord has given you the land, and that the fear of you has fallen upon us, and that all the inhabitants of the land melt away before you. For we have heard how the Lord dried up the water of the Red Sea before you when you came out of Egypt, and what you did to the two kings of the Amorites who were beyond the Jordan, to Sihon and Og, whom you devoted to destruction. And as soon as we heard it, our hearts melted, and there was no spirit left in any man because of you, for the Lord your God, he is God in the heavens above and on the earth beneath. Now then, please swear to me by the Lord that, as I have dealt kindly with you,

you also will deal kindly with my father's house, and give me a sure sign that you will save alive my father and mother, my brothers, and sisters, and all who belong to them, and deliver our lives from death." And the men said to her, "Our life for yours even to death! If you do not tell this business of ours, then when the Lord gives us the land we will deal kindly and faithfully with you."

Then she let them down by a rope through the window, for her house was built into the city wall so that she lived in the wall. And she said to them, "Go into the hills, or the pursuers will encounter you, and hide their three days until the pursuers have returned. Then afterward you may go your way." The men said to her, "We will be guiltless with respect to this oath of yours that you have made us swear. Behold, when we come into the land, you shall tie this scarlet cord in the window through which you let us down, and you shall gather into your house your father and mother, your brothers, and all your father's household. Then if anyone goes out of the doors of your house into the street, his blood shall be on his own head, and we shall be guiltless. But if a hand is laid on anyone who is with you in the house, his blood shall be on our head. But if you tell this business of ours, then we shall be guiltless with respect to your oath that you have made us swear." And she said, "According to your words, so be it." Then she sent them away, and they departed. And she tied the scarlet cord in the window.

The skin on my neck and arms tingled, and my heart skipped a beat as I studied the original word for "cord." Only God can give us such a gem. The word for "cord" in the original language is used often in the Old Testament: *chebel*, which means lace, bracelet, wire, twist, cord.

The book of Joshua is the only place *chebel* is replaced with the word *tiqvah*, which means "hope."

I stop and praise God every time I think of this. Hope is an integral theme of the Bible. "Though he slay me, I will hope in him" (Job 13:15).

For God alone, O my soul, wait in silence, for my hope is from him. (Psalm 62:5)

[A]nd hope does not put us to shame, because God's love has been poured into our hearts through the Holy Spirit who has been given to us. (Romans 5:5)

The chord (*tiqvah*) was a promise of freedom and purpose for her and her family, a fresh start to a new way of life.

The spies return trip took at least three weeks, plus a week of marching around the city. Rahab and her family had to wait. I don't know about you, but I get anxious waiting for microwave popcorn.

The Bible does not mention how Rahab and her family spent the time waiting. I am careful not to add to Scripture or fill in areas where God is silent. I do believe that while the spies were gone, Rahab looked out her window as she waited for the men to return and was fixated on the red chord—the promise of a new life. I wonder if her family got fidgety and ridiculed her. Have you had others question your motives as you wait for God's plan? Take heart! He will reveal his will to you.

Since Rahab had a window, I wondered if her excitement built when she saw Joshua and his men march toward the city. Did she grip the cord, knowing that hope would not disappoint?

Joshua and his army took Jericho, just as God promised.

Rahab and her family were rescued after the wall crashed in around them.

Imagine the family's fear when the wall fell around them. They were not hurt. I picture them huddled together in the middle of the room. God was with them in their fear. He sent Joshua and his men to rescue them from the rubble, and Rahab and her family found favor with the Israelites.

Rahab married Salmon. This prostitute never imagined that she would be part of history in the making. "[A]nd Salmon the father of Boaz by Rahab, and Boaz the father of Obed by Ruth, and Obed the father of Jesse, and Jesse the father of David the king" (Matthew 1:5–6).

Jesus is an offspring of David. "Remember Jesus Christ, risen from the dead, the offspring of David, as preached in my gospel" (2 Timothy 2:8).

Rahab, the prostitute, is in the lineage of Jesus. If God can use a prostitute, he can and will use us. We need not fear.

God took Rahab from the darkness of her sin and brought her into the light of redemption and purpose. She was used by God in a mighty way. I'm sure she was fearful at times, but she knew the power of her God and stood firm, even as her world collapsed around her.

She is recognized, along with Abraham, Moses, Gideon, Barak, Samson, Jephthah, David, Samuel, and the prophets, for her faith. "By faith Rahab the prostitute did not perish with those who were disobedient, because she had given a friendly welcome to the spies" (Hebrews 11:31).

The Bible includes many fearless men and women who shined for God. From Genesis to Revelation God proclaims, "Fear not!"

And the Lord appeared to him the same night and said, "I am the God of Abraham your father. Fear not, for I am with you and will bless you and multiply your offspring for my servant Abraham's sake." (Genesis 26:24)

Do not fear what you are about to suffer. Behold, the devil is about to throw some of you into prison, that you may be tested, and for ten days you will have tribulation. Be faithful unto death, and I will give you the crown of life. (Revelation 2:10)

As we apply the STAR principle to our lives, fear and worry will try to slither in like a snake gliding unnoticed to devour its prey. Let's be confident—fearless—because the resurrection power of Christ lives in us, and our heavenly Father is protecting us. God is love. Perfect love casts out all fear!

===========================

Memory verse
1 John 4:18, "There is no fear in love, but perfect love casts out fear."

Light reflection questions:

1. Why did Rahab have hope? Explain.

2. Why does God tell us not to fear? Explain.

3. What still causes fear in your life? How can you apply God's Word to eradicate dread?

Rise and Shine?

Reality is a thief. After eleven deaths of close friends and family within the span of one year, I despaired. How could I still shine and grieve at the same time when a cloud of sadness overwhelmed me? I remembered a conversation I had with my son.

"I miss grandpa," my son said with tears streaming down his face. "I wish he never died."

My heart broke as my son sobbed and hugged his bear. I missed him too. I prayed and asked God to give me the words to say.

"I also miss Grandma Colby and Terry, and I know you must miss Sue."

My fourteen-year-old son has experienced much loss over the last few year—all followers of Jesus.

As I hugged my son, the Spirit impressed upon my heart 2 Corinthians 5:8, where the apostle Paul states, "Yes, we are of good courage, and we would rather be away from the body and at home with the Lord."

I thought to myself, *In the Lord's presence, no one is dead. In fact, they are more alive than ever.*

"Michael, their bodies are in the ground, but their spirits are with Jesus. They are all more alive than ever. No cancer or Alzheimer's."

I silently thanked God for giving me the words to say to my grieving son. I too was encouraged, picturing my loved ones walking and talking with Jesus.

"Do you think they are talking to each other?" my autistic son said as he hugged his bear tighter.

"Yes, I bet grandma and Jesus are square dancing."

"I still miss them, Mom."

"It's OK to miss them, but they do not want us to fret because we will see them again."

"I can't wait to hug them and Jesus."

My son smiled and swirled his bear in the air; the bear danced.

Death will never have victory over a believer. But the absence of our loved ones still causes us to grieve deeply even if we desire to shine for God.

I did research on the word "shine." There are thirty-two verses in the ESV version of the Bible! Many of them are the like the blessing found in Numbers 6:25: "[T]he LORD make his face to shine upon you and be gracious to you."

I wanted to be in the presence of my God. I remember a time when I struggled with doubting that God was with me. Have you had this experience?

"You are welcome, O Lord. We invite you here to be with us and shine on us," the worship leader prayerfully sang.

Isn't he already here living in my heart? I asked myself.

As a new believer, I was confused. I heard my brothers and sisters inviting God or the Spirit to enter into the room.

Questions flooded my mind. *Isn't God omnipresent? Why do we need to invite him to be with us if he is already living inside us?*

Was King David wrong in praying, "Where shall I go from your Spirit? Or where shall I flee from your presence? If I ascend to heaven, you are there! If I make my bed in Sheol, you are there!" (Psalm 139:7–8)

Why do I hear, "We invite you God," when some pray or worship?

I asked a few people.

One person said, "Oh Cherrilynn, you don't have to be so literal."

Ouch! I'm literal when it comes to God.

Scripture revealed the truth. "The eyes of the Lord are in every place, keeping watch on the evil and the good" (Proverbs 15:3).

Can a man hide himself in secret places so that I cannot see him? declares the Lord. Do I not fill heaven and earth? declares the Lord. (Jeremiah 23:24)

Years later, while participating as a prayer partner at a Beth Moore conference, Beth said, "I don't invite God. He is already here. He invites us into his presence."

Thank you, Beth, for more confirmation.

God is everywhere; we need not invite him. He is waiting for us to acknowledge him and bask in his light, even when we are filled with grief. So how do I shine when I'm crushed in spirit and know that God is with me?

The blessing in Numbers 6:25 is important because the Old Testament priest declared it, and rabbis still quote it today. The blessing implies God does not shine on everyone. He causes his face to shine on those who seek him. The words "make his face shine on you" mean "may his presence be evident in you, may he leave a visible trace of his being on the face you show to others."

Even when we are sad, God can still shine in and through us. There are times we have no strength to read the Word, let alone concentrate on the STAR principle. The chains of sorrow bind us, and we feel the distress deep in our bones. What do we do? Paul and Silas were tortured for casting an evil spirit out of a woman.

The crowd joined in attacking them, and the magistrates tore the garments off them and gave orders to beat them with rods. And when they had inflicted many blows upon them, they threw them into prison, ordering the jailer to keep them safely. Having received this order, he put them into the inner prison and fastened their feet in the stocks. (Acts 16:22–24)

Imagine your clothes torn off, your body beat to a pulp, and you are thrown into a deep, dark, cold jail and put into shackles. The pain is unbearable as the shackles rub against your bleeding wounds. Perhaps others are heckling you.

Many of us have been in an emotional place that feels like jail, or perhaps you are there now. My dear brother or sister, when hope seems lost and the light appears nonexistent, the answer lies with Paul and Silas.

About midnight Paul and Silas were praying and singing hymns to God, and the prisoners were listening to them, and suddenly there was a great earthquake, so that the foundations of the prison were shaken. And immediately all the doors were opened, and everyone's bonds were unfastened. (Acts 16:25–26)

Now, when mourning darkens my heart and I'm weak, I sing praises to God. At first I don't feel like worshiping, but I think of Paul and Silas. I also think of Hebrews 13:15: "Through him then let us continually offer up a sacrifice of praise to God."

Our praise and worship is through the power of the Holy Spirit and may cost us. God is pleased when we cry out, "Hallelujah! Praise be to God!" especially when we don't feel like it.

Charles Spurgeon, known as the prince of preachers, said, "So, then, we are to utter the praises of God, and it is not sufficient to feel adoring emotions."

When your soul is downcast, sing "Hallelujah!" *Halal* means "to be clear," "to shine," "to make a show," "to boast in the Lord," "to be clamorously foolish."

Every time we praise the Lord, we shine. Have you watched believers worship? Their countenance glows.

Psalm 42 is titled "To the chief musician. A contemplation of the sons of Korah—a maskil." The sons of Korah were Levites, from the family of Kohath. In David's time, they served as the musicians at temple worship. Korah led a rebellion against Moses during the wilderness days of the Exodus. God judged Korah and his leaders and they all died, but the sons of Korah remained. Perhaps they were so grateful for God's mercy that they became notable in Israel for praising God. A *maskil* was meant to be sung and written to make people wise.

The title does not tell us who wrote this psalm, but most scholars believe David penned it at a time during Saul's persecution or Absalom's rebellion. David was driven from the sanctuary.

"Why are you cast down, O my soul, and why are you in turmoil within me? Hope in God; for I shall again praise him, my salvation." (Psalm 42:5)

David preached to his own soul. He did not submit to his feelings of depression and discouragement. He brought them before God. He said to his feelings, "Hope in God. He will come through again."

So when your soul is downcast, in need of hope—sing praises! "Oh come, let us sing to the LORD; let us make a joyful noise to the rock of our salvation!" (Psalm 95:1)

Make a joyful noise! God hears the melody of your heart, even if you sing out of tune!

Sing and shine!

===========================

Memory verse
Hebrews 13:15, "Through him then let us continually offer up a sacrifice of praise to God."

Light reflection questions:

1. What did David do to help with his depression?

2. What happened when Paul and Silas worshiped God in prison?

3. What is the definition of *halal*?

Shine Bright

Congratulations! We have journeyed through the STAR principle. Are there any recognizable changes in your life? I know God teaches me a new truth each time I revisit one of the principles. One of the biggest truths I learned is that no one is attracted to a whiner. Whiners live a lie. Truth is found when the STAR principles are manifest daily.

My journey from whine to shine was long, and after many years of God revealing the dark places in my heart, I felt different. A friend I had not seen in fifteen years confirmed it.

"Cherrilynn, you have changed," Sandy said.

"How?"

"I don't want to hurt your feelings, but you complained a lot, and now you don't. You have so much joy," Sandy said.

I briefly shared my story and how the STAR principle changed my whine to shine. "Do everything without grumbling or arguing, so that you may become blameless and pure, 'children of God without fault in a warped and crooked generation.' Then you will shine among them like stars in the sky" (Philippians 2:14–16 NIV).

We learned that we are here to serve him and shine our light into this dark world. The best part is that he gives us the power to illuminate the world. We are filled with his light—we have no reason to complain.

For you are all children of light, children of the day. We are not of the night or of the darkness. (1 Thessalonians 5:5)

[F]or at one time you were darkness, but now you are light in the Lord. Walk as children of light. (Ephesians 5:8)

If then your whole body is full of light, having no part dark, it will be wholly bright, as when a lamp with its rays gives you light. (Luke 11:36)

The purpose of the STAR principle is to change our darkness into his marvelous light.

Jesus said, "In the same way, let your light shine before others, so that they may see your good works and give glory to your Father who is in heaven." (Matthew 5:16)

Light is powerful!

In the beginning, God created light. Since the beginning of time, the evil one has wanted to be a god and has tried to create his own light. "And no wonder, for even Satan disguises himself as an angel of light" (2 Corinthians 11:14).

Satan tried to shoot his fiery arrow into a place where I was previously vulnerable. I was more aware of my weakness, yet Satan tried to use this gorgeous, charming man to seduce me, knowing my desire to be married. It was not just my flesh this time. I was overwhelmed with an attack of yearning. A supernatural cloud of darkness with a magnetic power engulfed me. My attraction to this man was something I hadn't felt before. It's difficult to explain, but I knew it was not godly. The man was relentless, telling me how beautiful I was, proclaiming to know Christ, and showed up wherever I went. Only through prayer and clinging to the Word could I break the spell. I stood firm in the armor. I called on Jesus to fight the battle, and this handsome deceiver's true colors were revealed. When he could not seduce me, he moved on to his next prey—another Christian woman. He left heartache and destruction in his wake. He destroyed a marriage and caused this woman to lose her job and children. Satan used him to try to carry out his devious plan. The battle was won because the light of Christ in me revealed the true intentions of this man and gave me the strength to overpower the darkness.

"Little children, you are from God and have overcome them, for he who is in you is greater than he who is in the world." (1 John 4:4)

The original Greek word for "light" is *phōs*. In this passage it means "of one in whom wisdom and spiritual purity shine forth, and who imparts the same to others."

Phōs is also used when referring to Satan being an angel of light. He is smart and has been studying mankind for thousands of years. However, the light of love extinguishes the imposters light of deception.

As I studied this word, I found that *phōs* also refers to the light emitted from a star.

See, we are stars shining in the universe, piercing the darkness.

The light of Christ stopped Paul on the road to Damascus. Paul wanted to bring Christians to Jerusalem and stone them. The light blinded Paul and stopped him from committing a heinous act against God. Jesus gave Paul a command to proclaim the good news "to open their eyes, so that they may turn from darkness to light and from the power of Satan to God, that they may receive forgiveness of sins and a place among those who are sanctified by faith in me."

The light of God in Paul pointed many to Jesus.

Many believers still struggle with darkness. You may still have chains of guilt and shame because you can't seem to get out of the prison cell. Don't let the evil one consume you with darkness. Look for the light.

I volunteered to pray for others at a Beth Moore conference. What I heard broke my heart.

"I'm addicted to sex; it's dishonoring to God as a single woman. Can God forgive me?" a woman told me as I held her hands to pray.

"My husband wants to leave because I'm fat; it's all my fault. I should exercise more," the next woman said as her thin figure stood before me.

"I can't stop eating; I am so depressed," a third woman confessed.

I left the conference burdened for these women. The angst they shared is common to believers. The darkness of lies blinded them from the beautiful light of Christ, and the light that resides inside them dimmed.

Paul the apostle wrestled with the darkness. We all will encounter gloom one or more times in our lives.

My brother or sister, if you are in a dark pit, I beseech you: don't fight the light. The purpose of light is not to cast shadows but to guide our steps and refine us to shine like a star. If you are in blatant sin, repent and live in the light of his forgiveness and glory. If you've been sinned against, forgive and allow God's love to heal you. It's not easy, but you can do anything with the resurrection power living inside you.

Paul was shipwrecked and left for dead. He learned to be content in all circumstances. He said, "But one thing I do: forgetting what lies behind and straining forward to what lies ahead, I press on toward the goal for the prize of the upward call of God in Christ Jesus" (Philippians 3:13–14).

Paul was stating that he was reaching forward, refusing to look back. He was determined to reach his goal by pursuing Christ. Paul wrote to the Roman church, "The night is far gone; the day is at hand. So then let us cast off the works of darkness and put on the armor of light." (Romans 13:12)

Job had everything taken away from him. He would not curse God. He did, however, question God. At the end of his trial Job said, "He has redeemed my soul from going down into the pit, and my life shall look upon the light.' 'Behold, God does all these things, twice, three times, with a man, to bring back his soul from the pit, that he may be lighted with the light of life" (Job 33:28–29).

Paul and Job knew the steadfast character of God. Each man endured intense suffering but turned to the light of God and continued to serve him.

Wholehearted service is not easy, especially when our light grows dim and the darkness creeps in due to the cares of this world. Let the light of God's love melt the sin, pain, and worry.

God is love and light.

Love ignites us to desire the transformation of our minds through his Word. He empowers us to love and serve others no matter the cost.

Love communicates with us, and in turn, we desire to bask in his presence, praising him and discussing our concerns and joys.

Love guides us through trials and tribulations; we understand nothing goes unseen by the lover of our souls.

Our goal should be to shine like Jesus. "And those who are wise shall shine like the brightness of the sky above; and those who turn many to righteousness, like the stars forever and ever" (Daniel 12:3).

We are his stars. "He counts the number of the stars; He calls them all by their names" (Psalm 147:4 AMP).

When you feel a whine in your heart, review the STAR principles, and always remember the words of the apostle Peter, "But you are a chosen race, a royal priesthood, a holy nation, a people for his own possession, that you may proclaim the excellencies of him who called you out of darkness into his marvelous light." (1 Peter 2:9)

=============================

Memory verse
Luke 11:36, "If then your whole body is full of light, having no part dark, it will be wholly bright, as when a lamp with its rays gives you light."

Light reflection questions:

1. What is the Greek word for "light?"

2. What is the definition of this word?

3. Explain why a star is similar to this word.

Shine, Don't Whine Memory Verses

The Pit of Perfection
Galatians 5:1 NASB
"It was for freedom that Christ set us free; therefore keep standing firm and do not be subject again to a yoke of slavery."

Attitude Adjustment
Philippians 2:14–16 NIV
"Do everything without grumbling or arguing, so that you may become blameless and pure, 'children of God without fault in a warped and crooked generation.' Then you will shine among them like stars."

S: See Yourself as God Sees You
Ephesians 1:4
"[E]ven as he [God] chose us in him [Jesus] before the foundation of the world, that we should be holy and blameless before him."

Before Salvation
Colossians 1:21
"And you, who once were alienated and hostile in mind, doing evil deeds."

After Salvation
1 Corinthians 6:19b–20
"You are not your own, for you were bought with a price. So glorify God in your body."

Saved to Serve
Matthew 20:28

"[E]ven as the Son of Man came not to be served but to serve, and to give his life as a ransom for many."

T: Transformed Mind
Ephesians 4:22–23 (NIV)

"[Y]ou were taught with regard to your former way of life to put off your old self which is being corrupted by deceitful desires to be made new in the attitude of your minds."

Feelings Versus Truth
Isaiah 6:7

"And he touched my mouth and said: 'Behold, this has touched your lips; your guilt is taken away, and your sin atoned for.'"

Work the Word
Ephesians 4:22–23

"[T]o put off your old self, which belongs to your former manner of life and is corrupt through deceitful desires, and to be renewed in the spirit of your minds."

Memorize the Word
Psalm 119:11

"I have stored up your word in my heart, that I might not sin against you."

A: Always Pray
Acts 6:4

"But we will devote ourselves to prayer and to the ministry of the word."

Journalistic Approach
Psalm 116:2

"Because he inclined his ear to me, therefore I will call on him as long as I live."

Surgical Prayer
Romans 5:5

"[A]nd hope does not put us to shame, because God's love has been poured into our hearts through the Holy Spirit who has been given to us."

Pray the Armor
Romans 13:12

"The night is far gone; the day is at hand. So then let us cast off the works of darkness and put on the armor of light."

R: Refined to Shine
Proverbs 20:30

"Blows that wound cleanse away evil;
strokes make clean the innermost parts."

Expect Trials
John 16:33

"In the world you will have tribulation. But take heart; I have overcome the world."

Refined to Shine
2 Corinthians 4:17–18

"For this light momentary affliction is preparing for us an eternal weight of glory beyond all comparison, as we look not to the things that are seen but to the things that are unseen."

Shine for Salvation
Daniel 12:3

"And those who are wise shall shine like the brightness of the sky above; and those who turn many to righteousness, like the stars forever and ever."

Shine On

Matthew 5:16

"In the same way, let your light shine before others, so that they may see your good works and give glory to your Father who is in heaven."

Fearless Light

1 John 4:18

"There is no fear in love, but perfect love casts out fear."

Rise and Shine?

Hebrews 13:15

"Through him then let us continually offer up a sacrifice of praise to God."

Shine Bright

Luke 11:36

"If then your whole body is full of light, having no part dark, it will be wholly bright, as when a lamp with its rays gives you light."

Printed in the United States
By Bookmasters